Bugles, Boots, and Saddles

Bugles, Boots, and Saddles

EXPLOITS OF THE U.S. CAVALRY

Edited by Stephen Brennan

Skyhorse Publishing

All rights reserved. No part of this book may be reproduced in any manner without the express written consent of the publisher, except in the case of brief excerpts in critical reviews or articles. All inquiries should be addressed to Skyhorse Publishing, 307 West 36th Street, 11th Floor, New York, NY 10018.

Skyhorse Publishing books may be purchased in bulk at special discounts for sales promotion, corporate gifts, fund-raising, or educational purposes. Special editions can also be created to specifications. For details, contact the Special Sales Department, Skyhorse Publishing, 307 West 36th Street, 11th Floor, New York, NY 10018 or info@skyhorsepublishing.com.

Skyhorse® and Skyhorse Publishing® are registered trademarks of Skyhorse Publishing, Inc.®, a Delaware corporation.

Visit our website at www.skyhorsepublishing.com.

10 9 8 7 6 5 4 3 2 1

Library of Congress Cataloging-in-Publication Data is available on file.

Cover design by Rain Saukas

Cover painting: *On the Southern Plains* by Frederic Remington; The Metropolitan Museum of Art

Print ISBN: 978-1-5107-0448-0
Ebook ISBN: 978-1-5107-0449-7

Printed in United States of America

Boots and Saddles: The bugle call for cavalry troops to mount and to take their place in the line.

Contents

Introduction

In his time, many people considered George Washington to be the best horseman in the colonies. It's odd, then, that in the first days of our Revolutionary War, it looked as though he was determined to dispense with the use of mounted troops altogether. When, in the early summer of 1776, Washington moved his rabble of an army to New York City, he faced two primary tasks. Most immediately, he needed to defend the city from a British invasion that everyone knew was coming, and perhaps more importantly, he needed to organize, supply, discipline, and deploy an army that would be capable of taking the field against King George's troops, which were considered to be the best in the world.

Building an army had not been easy and by midsummer it was still very much a work in progress. The various regional militias and other largely ad hoc forces under Washington's command were mostly insubordinate, mistrustful of one another, jealous each of their particular prerogatives, and uncertain in a fight. But Washington soon understood that if this ragtag force was to be the means by which the colonists secured their independence, he would have to rethink the whole concept of what it meant to be a military commander. To this end, the general swallowed his pride and instead of simply issuing orders, he adopted a policy of at once flattering and cajoling—and only occasionally bullying—his recalcitrant troops.

By early July, Washington had begun to make some progress along these lines when a large company of mounted troops—five hundred or so—arrived at his headquarters. They had come from Connecticut, and they had been raised and organized from among the patriot gentry. Most of them were well off, and many traveled with their own servants and were accompanied by a string of spare mounts. Their uniforms were gorgeous. At first, Washington was nonplussed. This was not, he felt, what he needed to defend New York. His army required arms, infantry, powder, and rations, not this horde of gentlemen cavaliers. More than that, their mere presence threatened to upset all his arrangements and stratagems, the careful balance between the egos and prejudices of his disparate force. Therefore, his first gambit was to declare that unfortunately he had no forage for the horses and no funds with which to procure any. No worries, replied the cavaliers, who explained that they were men of property who would buy the forage themselves. But when the General further informed them that he required them to serve as dismounted troops, to join the line and help dig fortifications, they took themselves back to Connecticut in some haste.

Washington's own prior experience was in backwoods fighting, where the mounted warrior had little role to play. The real difficulty was that he—as well as most of the other American commanders—had scant insight regarding the war-making potential of mounted troops, much less any idea of the value of an arm of the service specifically organized for the purposes of shock-attack and pursuit, reconnaissance and exploration, screening an advance or a retreat, and harassing an enemy himself in retreat. Eventually, Washington and his officers grew to understand something of their value, and over the next one hundred years, the U.S. Cavalry adapted itself to the needs and imperatives of the growing nation, often covering itself in glory and only occasionally miring itself in shame.

As the whole history of the U.S. Cavalry is too immense a subject for any one volume, this book is composed largely of accounts and memoirs of officers and men who served in the various actions and theaters of conflict. The aim is toward an impressionistic effect, each exploit giving color and contrast to the whole.

Besides the virtue of being primary source history, each exploit illustrates unique aspects of U.S. Cavalry life and tactics in the nineteenth century.

—Stephen Brennan
Cornwall, CT
2016

Classic U.S. Cavalry Arms, Tactics, and Practices

This first section of the book is here offered as an introduction to the whole world of the U.S. Cavalry trooper in the nineteenth century. Materials are freely edited and adapted from Cavalry Tactics as Illustrated by the War of the Rebellion, *by Alonzo Gray;* History of the United States Cavalry, *by Albert G. Bracket; and* Across the Continent with the Fifth Cavalry, *by George F. Price.*

Arms

American Revolutionary War dragoons were armed with saber and horse pistols. The mounted riflemen fought dismounted and were armed with long rifles and knives or hatchets.

During the Mexican War, the dragoons were armed with musketoons, which were carried on sling belts. They also carried dragoon sabers of Prussian pattern and horse pistols.

The Mounted Rifles were armed with percussion rifles and Colt army revolvers but no sabers.

Civil War cavalry regiments were armed with sabers, rifle-carbines and Colt navy revolvers.

During the Civil War, the U.S. Cavalry was generally armed with short breech-loading rifles or carbines, sabers, and revolvers. The short rifles carried at the commencement of the Civil War were later replaced by carbines, and the single-loading carbines were, in the later part of the war, replaced by repeating ones.

At the beginning of the Civil War, the sabers were of the Prussian pattern, with a long, straight blade. These were soon replaced by the light cavalry saber with a curved blade, which was much more highly regarded than the Prussian saber.

The Colt revolver was generally carried. It was loaded with powder and ball, and fired with a percussion cap.

The year 1861 saw the raising of the Sixth Pennsylvania, the only regiment of lancers ever fielded by the U.S. Cavalry, but this regiment exchanged the lance for the saber in April 1863. Although American troops had faced British lancers in the Revolutionary War and in the War of 1812, and very skillful lancers in the Mexican War, this method of fighting never really caught on in the U.S. From time to time, there were experiments with its use but nothing much came of them. This was largely because the lance could not be used to good advantage in the close, wooded country found everywhere along the Atlantic coast and in the eastern states generally. By the time of the Indian Wars following the Civil War—fought mostly in the open country of the Great Plains and the deserts of the Southwest—advances in the firepower of the carbine and the revolver obviated any need for the mounted lancer.

Saber Versus Revolver

Throughout the nineteenth century, there was a great deal of discussion in the U.S. Cavalry service regarding the relative merits of the revolver and saber. This discussion was time wasted. Each weapon had its distinct and proper uses, and neither could replace the other.

During the Civil War—just as it had been throughout the history of the mounted warrior—the saber was the essential weapon for shock action. But in individual combat—one man pitted against another—the revolver was to be the winner in almost every case. If the trooper were expert in its use and his luck held, he had little to fear from an individual enemy armed with a saber.

During the thick of the melee that followed impact, the saber was still preferred; but when the melee devolved into individual combat, the saber was most often exchanged for the revolver. Since the switch from saber to revolver was made during the fight, the trooper had to be able to get his weapon into action rapidly. This exchange of weapons was accomplished either by discarding the saber altogether, or by returning it to its scabbard, or by dropping it and letting it hang attached to the wrist by a sword knot. The first option was really no option at all, as it involved the loss of the weapon; the second method was nearly impossible when in motion; the third meant some danger to the trooper or to his mount—especially if the weapon was as sharp as it should be. Thus, there was no really satisfactory way to swap the saber for the revolver while in action.

The revolver on the right hip also had a yard-long cord fastened to it. The troopers were practiced in firing at a target while passing at speed and then dropping the pistol on the opposite side, letting it hang by the cord while they handled the saber.

The true use of the revolver lay in irregular warfare, where single, man-to-man combats and sudden encounters of small parties took place—on horseback, in narrow lanes, among woods and fences—where the saber could not be used. In such places, and wherever regular order was broken up, the revolver was invaluable. In pursuits, patrols, and surprises, it was superior to the saber.

The revolver or pistol—a large-caliber weapon with great stopping power, quick firing, and accurate up to about fifty yards—was used whenever regular order was broken up. That is, in individual combat, charging as foragers on wagon trains or artillery, in the woods, on patrol duty, when on a mounted skirmish line in close country, and in irregular or partisan warfare where sudden encounters of small parties were to be expected. In a melee, the carbine was useless against the revolver. The revolver was also sometimes used for collective fire while dismounted but, ideally, only under exceptional circumstances, such as from behind a stone wall or for defense after the carbine ammunition had become exhausted.

The Cavalry Charge

It was often asserted that the horse was the real weapon in the charge and that it made little difference whether a trooper had a revolver or saber in his hand, but the moral effect of the flash and glitter of a "three-foot razor" was not to be ignored.

In fact, the psychological impact of the charge was tremendous. The fierce charging yell, rising and swelling higher and higher until it overtopped the sound of musketry, frightened men more than bullets did, and few troops would stand up against a cavalry charge if they were unsupported by works—out in the open and away from fortifications such as stone walls or entrenchments. In line charges in the open field, the saber most often conquered.

The troopers were taught never to fire before the command. The effect of this *reserved volley* was telling. Irregular firing during an advance by mounted troops proved useless and demoralizing. The time to fire was thirty or forty feet from the enemy's line, all together and aiming low. Troopers were cautioned never to try long shots when attacking on horseback.

The general practice from the time of the Mexican War was that the charge should be made at a *raise saber*—i.e., with the sword held above the head—and this continued to be the case all through the 1840s and well into the Civil War.

Commanders found that their men used it no matter what was officially prescribed and that untrained men instinctively used the saber as they would use a club. Furthermore, since the effect of the saber before and at the instant of contact or shock is largely a moral one, it seemed that this effect would be materially increased by carrying the saber during the charge at a *raise saber* rather than at the position of *charge saber* or *tierce point*, since in the former position, with its flash and glitter, its effect would be much greater than if carried at the latter. Despite this, by the 1860s cavalry tactics prescribed the *tierce point* as the approved posture for charging cavalry troops. The common practice was to begin the charge with the troopers holding their sabers point forward at *tierce* and change them to *raise saber* about fifty yards out.

Analects of Classic Cavalry Tactics and Practices of the Civil War Era
Fire Action
Anything that encourages men to "charge home" doubles their morale, and morale is everything.

Cavalry, in falling back, needs to be careful to move to the flanks of supporting infantry; otherwise, their confusion is communicated to the infantry with serious consequences to the latter.

If possible, a charge should always be met by a charge.

The charge will be most destructive if the enemy can be caught in the act of maneuvering.

A mounted column should always be held in readiness to take the initiative when opportunity is offered. At rare intervals, there will be a golden moment and the commander who would seize it must be found ready.

Ground scouts should always be sent in advance of attacking troops.

Reserves should have sabers drawn.

Care must be exercised that cavalry does not arrive at the charging point in a distressed or "blown" condition. The distance over which cavalry can travel at an increased gait and still be fit to deliver a shock will depend upon their training. Frederick the Great required that his cavalry be able to pass over four thousand yards at a trot and eighteen hundred yards at a gallop, and still be able to finish three hundred to four hundred yards at full speed. Modern conditions involving long-range firearms make it more essential than ever that cavalry are able to pass over great distances at high speed.

The saber was frequently used as the charging weapon against artillery. However, the best results will be obtained by using the revolver, since the gunners will take refuge behind their pieces and can execute well with the revolvers with which they are armed. A frontal charge against artillery is not likely to succeed unless the distance is very short; the greater the distance charged, the less the chance of success. In this case, the flank attack offers a fair chance of success unless the artillery is well supported by foot troops.

The frontal attack on artillery with mounted troops in the center and dismounted troops on the flanks is an example of the poorest kind of tactic.

The best time to strike artillery is when it is in the act of limbering or unlimbering. (Artillery was moved from place to place by horse-drawn caissons—two-wheeled wagons containing ammunition and other gear. *Limbering* a gun means to attach it to, and stow the ammunition and gear in, the caisson, so that it can be moved. *Unlimbering* a gun means to separate it from the caisson and move it into firing position.)

Fire Action Against Infantry

It is now generally accepted that unshaken infantry cannot be successfully charged in front by cavalry. This is not necessarily true. The infantry of Frederick the Great in solid lines, three deep, delivered a fire of fifty-caliber balls as rapidly as our thin lines, with two-yard intervals, can now deliver a fire of thirty-caliber bullets. In Frederick's time, every ball that hit a horse stopped it. Unless hit in a vital spot by a thirty-caliber bullet, a horse with many wounds will now finish the charge and still be able to leave the field. There will be many opportunities offered for a successful charge against infantry other than directly against its front. It can be charged in flank; when changing front; while forming; while in column emerging from a defile or from the woods; when shaken by fire; and in a canyon where it cannot deploy.

If infantry can be surprised by a well-executed charge, it is likely that its fire will be very inaccurate.

It will often be possible to support a mounted charge by dismounted fire or the fire of artillery delivered from a flank position; this will keep down the enemy's fire and divert it from the charging troops.

When dismounted, troops break through a firing line, their advance may be checked by a mounted charge.

As soon as the leading unit has delivered its shock, it should rally in rear of the column. This exercise should be practiced frequently.

The more solid the mass at the instant of impact, the greater will be the effect of the shock. The charge should, therefore, be made boot-to-boot. Notwithstanding this well-known maxim, the tendency is to open out the rank at a time when the troopers' greatest safety lies in riding well closed toward the enemy.

If the three-line formation is used, the first line should usually be heavier than either the support or the reserve. If time is precious and success depends upon one cast of the die, the first line should be as strong as possible; if the enemy has reserves constantly arriving, then numerous lines should be used.

The lines should be far enough apart so that, if the advance line is beaten, it will not communicate its confusion to the lines in rear. For this reason, it is better to hold the troops in rear of the second lines of columns. The first line should be preceded by mounted skirmishers employing mounted rifle fire. These mounted skirmishers amount to the same thing as ground scouts, who would be sent out from troops in the front line.

After a line has been launched in a charge, the commander can only influence the fight by the use of troops held in reserve. The commander should not personally engage in the fight until after his last reserve is thrown in.

Mounted carbine fire was often used. This was confined mostly to mounted skirmishers who preceded the first line while forming for attack. It can also be used to accelerate the retreat of defeated infantry but should not replace the saber, which is more effective. The fire of mounted men is very inaccurate, since one hand is always necessary to control the horse.

Mounted carbine fire is not as accurate as revolver fire, provided the force armed with the revolvers comes to close quarters.

A badly defeated cavalry unit, if vigorously pursued with the revolver, will not stop running until it reaches the next county.

The mobility of cavalry renders it extremely valuable as a reinforcement to weak points in the line of battle.

A rapidly moving target does not suffer heavy losses.

Dismounted Fire Action

From behind a fence, troops shoot with greater accuracy than when in the open.

Dismounted men can often stop a mounted charge with their fire, even though it gets as close as 50 yards.

A formation for attack is strengthened by placing regular troops on the flanks.

The time for a skirmish line to go forward is when it receives fresh troops from the reserves.

Dismounted fire, when each man holds his horse by the reins, is very rare.

The time to inflict severe losses on an enemy is when his attacking line breaks to the rear.

Dismounted fire action will be resorted to when the ground is unsuited to mounted action.

Successful turning movements may be made for the purpose of attacking the flank or rear of an infantry line.

The fire of an attacking line should not be opened until the enemy's fire compels it.

At times, cavalry will be called upon to fight for long periods on foot. Breastworks—i.e., field fortifications—will often be constructed by cavalry with a view of their being occupied later by infantry.

Ammunition in boxes can be conveniently distributed along the line from pack mules before the action begins.

It will rarely be possible for cavalry to select a battlefield and hold it until occupied by infantry but it will often be possible for cavalry to hold important tactical positions until relieved by infantry. Under these conditions, the commander should see that the cavalry is not kept to do infantry work but is returned to its own legitimate sphere of usefulness.

Combined Mounted and Dismounted Action

In combined mounted and dismounted actions, with few exceptions, the dismounted men were in the center and the mounted men on the flanks. The exception is where the most suitable ground for a charge is along a narrow lane, running at right angles and leading to the center of the enemy's line, along which the charge will necessarily be made in column of fours. The reason for the mounted men being on the flanks is that by rapid movements they can attack or threaten the enemy's flanks and rear. If the enemy breaks, it will be difficult for them to regain their led horses, provided that the mounted men are quick to move aggressively.

Mounted troops should always be ready to charge when the enemy's line breaks.

When the enemy is broken, he should not be given time to form new lines with his reserve.

Dismounted sharpshooters under cover are a good support for a weak or timid mounted force.

If the terrain is not suited to retiring (i.e., orderly retreat) by successive formations, then the retreating dismounted men should be covered by mounted troops whose threatening attitude will give the dismounted men time to regain their horses.

When mounted, troops meet in a lane, the head of the column should engage in mounted combat, while those in rear break through the fences to the right and left, and endeavor to gain a flank fire on the rear of the enemy's column.

In a lane from which no deployment can be made, a small force may be considered equal to a large one as long as this condition can be maintained.

The tactical action of combined cavalry and infantry is much the same as that of mounted and dismounted cavalry.

Dismounted cavalry is often thrown into battle to strengthen infantry.

Cavalry should not believe that a lot of infantry must follow it around like the tail of a comet. The correct idea is expressed by Philip Sheridan, namely, that cavalry ought to fight the enemy's cavalry, and infantry the enemy's infantry. It is true that cavalry, like artillery, is a subordinate arm, and under the commanding general, should work to the overall plan for defeating an enemy, and while doing so, can and will fight anything. Good cavalry is, however, too difficult to replace to expend it on foot troops massed behind entrenchments and its potential is likewise too great to hinder its mobility by tying it to infantry support.

Cavalry can often cover the withdrawal of infantry by being placed in trenches, thus enabling the infantry to get away without molestation or its absence being discovered.

Cavalry will act as support for infantry more often than infantry acts as support for cavalry.

Putting cavalry into trenches for longer than twenty-four hours is very demoralizing to the cavalry. The fighting of men in the trenches will not, as a rule, compensate for the damage to their horses resulting from neglect.

Dismounted cavalry is particularly fitted for the work of delaying the advance of a victorious army. Its mobility enables it to take advantage of the terrain in places where its horses can be kept close up. Under this condition, it can delay its retirement with impunity, being able to retreat more quickly than infantry and thus being better at fighting rearguard actions. If horses cannot be kept close up, and owing to unfavorable terrain are sent to the rear, cavalry will still have an advantage over foot troops in that they carry no packs and are motivated by the assurance of safety upon regaining their horses.

The usual method of withdrawing was by alternate successive formations. It is possible, at times, to pit the whole fight on one good, strong position. In this case, when the smash comes, it will be every man for himself.

It will frequently happen that when circumstances, not known to the firing line, render a retirement desirable, a successful retirement may be made under cover of the confusion caused by a vigorous cavalry attack.

In the attack of a ford or bridge, the whole trick consists in keeping down the enemy's fire until the crossing can be managed and a deployment made on the opposite side. This may be done by rifle fire, artillery fire, or both combined. The method of employing it will depend upon the ground. If high banks overlook the crossing, position fire is desirable. Often a bold clash will turn the trick. This method is particularly applicable where the defenders can be surprised. One other method will often be possible, namely, delivering a vigorous attack and crossing under cover of the confusion caused to the enemy's ranks. But when the defense is strong, the enemy will suffer more by permitting his column to get well into the stream.

The cutting loose of one end of a pontoon bridge was also resorted to by Lee's army when crossing the Potomac after the Battle of Gettysburg.

Usually, some method can be found by which a crossing can be turned. The mobility of cavalry will enable it to reconnoiter, in a short time, a considerable distance to both flanks of the crossing, while other troops are engaging the enemy's attention in front. If a crossing can be found, it will be cheaper to turn the position than to force it.

Miscellaneous Tactics

A commander is not justified in withdrawing from a fight until he has put all his reserves into the firing line.

When Sheridan took command of the cavalry of the Army of the Potomac, he found the horses had been worn out by doing picket duty around an infantry camp on a line of nearly sixty miles, while the Confederates habitually sent their horses to the rear in winter to recuperate.

The use of cavalry as supply train guards is not to be encouraged. It is a great waste of cavalry and besides, the duty can be better performed by infantry. In case of an attack, the infantryman can shoot much more effectively than can a man on a horse. The speed of a train being much slower than the march of cavalry, it is very wearing on horses to hold them down to the rate of travel of the train.

The marching of cavalry in rear of infantry trains means that there will be nothing left for the cavalry to eat. When this condition is combined with night marching, the situation could not be worse for a cavalry command.

A very poor opinion is held of night operations. Their chief use will be limited to an attack over a short space of ground directly to the front after the troops have worked into position by daylight. Another application will be where the troops can work into position under the cover of darkness and make the attack at daybreak.

The size of an advance guard for a corps should be one brigade. On the point, it should be an advance guard of a sergeant and two men with connecting files extending back for a mile, one hundred yards apart—then about thirty men with connecting files for another mile—all totaling about seventy men. In this way, signals can be transmitted back two miles in two minutes. On each side road, the leading man rides out a quarter-mile or more and all the connecting files move up. When the last file is deployed, the lookout takes his place in rear. The employment of flankers and skirmishers, unless the enemy is known to be near, hardly pays for the consumption of horseflesh occasioned by constantly riding over broken ground. The flanking should be done by scouts, who travel light.

The subjects of security and reconnaissance are distinctly different. Security embraces advance, rear and flank guards, outposts and screening; while information embraces all kinds of reconnaissance, the employment of a spy and scout system, and the strategic use of cavalry.

Security will usually serve troops on the defensive while reconnaissance and the strategic use of cavalry will usually involve them in combat.

The defeat of the enemy's cavalry may prevent it from gaining information about the main body that is following.

An offensive screen will naturally result from a cavalry fight just preceding a battle and not far from the main body.

The formations used by cavalry on screening duty—whose aim is to screen or shield an army's movements and dispositions from its enemy—will necessarily be different from those used when seeking information. In screening, cavalry may be disposed so that if the enemy approaches, the screen, in falling back, gathers strength as it retires; while the cavalry, seeking the information, will try to break the screen and locate the enemy's main body. In order to do this, patrols may be sent out, which will endeavor to locate the weak points in the screen. The aggressors can then concentrate their forces in an effort to break the screen at its weak point, leaving the duty of screening their own forces to the divisional cavalry.

Screening means separation, while the penetration of an enemy's screen means concentration.

If the outpost used in a defensive screen is well out, care should be exercised that byroads do not enter behind the outpost.

Cavalry formations should remain on outpost duty until the infantry outposts are posted. Cavalry should then be brought in behind the infantry lines. If this is not done, the horses will all be rendered unserviceable by excessive work in a very short time. It is best to leave out only enough horses to patrol in front of the infantry outpost. The divisional cavalry may be sent out again early in the morning to take up the duties of the infantry while the latter is withdrawn.

The use of cavalry as a flank guard for other troops most frequently occurs while on the march.

In battle, cavalry will frequently be found on the flank of infantry either as a support or as a part of the firing line. Its mobility and its presence on the flanks will check any turning movement by the hostile cavalry.

Scouts and Spies

Scouts should go in pairs, they should be well mounted, leave sabers and packs with the baggage train, and live off the country. A well-organized scout organization should be kept at headquarters. They should not dress in the enemy's uniform. Their horses should be shod with rubber pad shoes.

The information obtained from independent cavalry by strategic reconnaissance is much more accurate and valuable than that obtained from civilians. The former will be trained military observers, while the latter, under stress of excitement, will either not know or terribly exaggerate. Occasionally intelligent citizens will be found who, in a systematic way, go about the matter of observing an enemy passing through a town and succeed in getting a report to the general of their own forces.

The information obtained from spies will be more or less valuable, depending upon the reliability of the spy, his intelligence and his opportunity for observation. Even a spy who plays double may be utilized.

A well-organized scouting system should be maintained in every army. All officers should be trained in the matter of estimating the number of troops seen. Autumn maneuvers (i.e., activities undertaken at the end of the campaign season as the army goes into winter quarters) furnish an excellent opportunity to make an application of this valuable accomplishment. A number of officers should be detailed daily to observe and report on the number of troops seen.

It is desirable to send important reports in duplicate to different superiors. Each report should mention the fact that a duplicate has been sent to the other superior.

A commander who hastily acts on information without seeking to verify it will usually make a mistake.

It will always be necessary to have a bureau of information at headquarters, where different reports can be compared and conclusions drawn from the multitude of reports received.

The absence of information is as much a handicap to a commander as the possession of it is an advantage.

When contact with the enemy is achieved, the cavalry should not lose it again.

Strategic Use of Cavalry

Cavalry that sticks close to the main body of the Army loses half its strength. It must be employed on distant expeditions to cut the enemy's lines, to be worth its cost in strategic combinations. For its full strategic effect, cavalry is obliged to live off the land after the first three days.

Cavalry operating strategically will be on the offensive and a considerable distance from its main body, while the opposing cavalry will be defensively screening its own forces.

Cavalry operating strategically will endeavor to break through the enemy's screen and observe the numbers and disposition of the enemy.

Cavalry can be screening defensively and while using good strategy will not be strategically used. Cavalry performing a defensive role may take the offensive and thus be used strategically. A forced reconnaissance amounts to a strategic use.

The strategic use of cavalry requires great activity, watchfulness and good judgment on the part of the commander.

Tactical use may also involve the use of strategy. A successful raid may be merged with strategic use depending upon the object of the raid.

Although cavalry strategically used might not get all the desired information, it might assist the commander's plans so as to produce great tactical results.

When cavalry, on a strategic mission, obtains valuable information, a staff officer should be sent with it to the commanding general. The messenger will then be able to answer questions and make explanations, thus elucidating matters that would otherwise remain obscure to the commanding general.

Pursuit

It is desirable to have a well-organized mounted force ready to take up the pursuit in case of victory. Flanking columns should take up the pursuit on parallel roads, endeavoring to cut in on the enemy's column, while troops following in rear endeavor to compel the enemy to deploy as frequently as possible. Only the parallel pursuit can meet with great results when cavalry is pursuing cavalry.

Fresh infantry can pursue defeated infantry but exhausted infantry cannot. In this case, cavalry is necessary.

The distance that a pursuit should be kept up will depend upon the progress of the general engagement. If cavalry defeats cavalry at the beginning of a battle, they should not pursue to the extent of becoming disorganized, but should rally and be kept in readiness to contribute to the general result. A decisive cavalry victory would amount to nothing if the general engagement is lost. If an enemy is defeated in a general engagement, there should be no limit to the pursuit. In that case, push it as far and as long as possible.

Raids

To be successful, a raid will have to be started without much preparation. If suspected by the enemy, it will not succeed. A strong diversion should be made in its favor.

Raids are seldom worth their cost in horseflesh and the damage done to the cavalry will be to the detriment of the raiders.

If the raiders cannot rejoin in safety, the raid may be counted as a failure.

Successful raids will generally be made in a friendly country or at least in a country where many sympathizers are found to give information.

Colonial Horse Soldiers

The following sections are adapted from the writings of Charles Francis Adams, Jr.

Revolutionary War Cavalry

Some years ago, I was accidentally led into a somewhat careful as well as critical examination of the actual facts of a Revolutionary battle, that before Brooklyn, N.Y., known as the Battle of Long Island, fought August 27, 1776. My attention was particularly drawn to the curious fact, which I did not remember ever to have seen noticed, that Washington, in the operations he then conducted, apparently had no conception of the use to be made of cavalry, or mounted men in warfare. His idea of an effective military organization, at least as he understood it, appeared to be a command consisting of infantry of the line, with a suitable artillery contingent. He did not seem at all to grasp the idea of some mounted force as an instrument essential to ascertaining the whereabouts and movements of his opponent, or concealing his own movements—or if it occurred to him, it was in a theoretical way, and not as a necessary means of meeting a present exigency.

Campaign of 1776

This is especially noticeable to any reader who might have had some practical experience in warfare, and most of all to one who has seen actual cavalry service. But it never seems to have occurred to the authors of most of our popular histories that in 1776 and later the seat of warfare in America, especially between the Hudson and the Potomac—the field in which Washington conducted his operations—was one singularly adapted to irregular cavalry operations. It was a region full of horses, while every Virginian and nearly every inhabitant of Pennsylvania and the Jerseys was accustomed to the saddle. People owned their mounts. Every farming lad and every son of a farmer was, in a rude way, an equestrian; the doctors made their rounds on horseback; the lawyers rode the circuits; in fact, the whole social and business life of the community was in a more or less direct way connected with the saddle. The horses, also, were of fairly good breed; and when brought into military use, showed solid powers of endurance.

This omission first becomes noticeable in connection with the narrative of events in the second year of the war—the operations in and about New York during the latter half of 1776. Prior to that time warfare had been waged on principles and by methods that were in every sense of the term irregular. Carried on in heavily wooded regions, it was a conflict between individuals, a struggle in which the ranger and rifleman were pitted against the savage or the Frenchman. In operations, except as couriers, the mounted man played no part. Even scouting was impracticable in a wilderness where an opponent might be lurking behind every cover. This held good through all the earlier Revolutionary operations from Concord and Lexington to the transfer of the scene of operations from the neighborhood of Boston to that of New York. Paul Revere, for instance, was mounted; but, when arrested in his ride, he was acting as a courier. Montgomery and Arnold led detachments into Canada, but their movements, when not by canoe, were made through a wilderness, pathless, and for the mounted man impracticable. So, from the beginning of American civilization down to August 1776, it may be said generally that, except as a pack animal or for draft and courier purposes, the horse found no place in military operations. Cavalry was not a recognized branch of the service. In the early months of 1776 the seat of active Revolutionary warfare was transferred from Boston and its immediate neighborhood to the mouth of the Hudson.

It was then apparent that to advance the patriot cause a wholly new system of strategy and tactics became advisable. The mouth of the Hudson did not, under conditions existing at the time, admit of successful defense. The better policy to be pursued was to abandon it to the enemy; and then to draw that enemy away from his base, into the interior, where the tactics of Lexington and Concord could be applied. Away from New York, the enemy would have no strategic objective, and he could be harassed day and night, from behind every tree and stonewall, holding only the ground on which he camped. The more country he tried to cover the more vulnerable he would have become.

Under these conditions, not yet developed fully, during the early days of July, and seven weeks before Sir William Howe showed any signs of activity, Governor Trumbull of Connecticut sent a detachment of "light-horse," as they were called, to New York. Some four or five hundred in number, they were a body of picked men, and as Washington wrote, "most of them, if not all, men of reputation and property."

Yet, because of the cost of forage, he refused to allow them to keep their horses, and, when they declined to do infantry duty, he roughly sent them home, writing to their commander, "They can no longer be of use here, where horses cannot be brought into action, and I do not care how soon they are dismissed." It is not easy to understand how a commander of even Washington's relative inexperience, under the conditions then confronting him, could have reached such a conclusion, much less have expressed it so bluntly and in writing. What did he have in mind when he asserted that his operations were necessarily conducted "where horses" could not "be brought into action?" It is true that both New York and Brooklyn were on islands, but that fact notwithstanding, the field of operations on those islands afforded ample space as well as constant occasion for the employment of any arm of the service, engineers, infantry, artillery or cavalry. Also, to hold the town of New York it was necessary to occupy Brooklyn, and the occupation of Brooklyn involved at least a dozen miles of uncovered front, or avenues of approach. These needed to be vigilantly guarded and patrolled. It was by means of one of these avenues of approach to Brooklyn, wholly unguarded, though only some four or five miles to the eastward of the direct road from the place where Howe landed his army, that a little later on, a detachment of the British force worked its way by a flanking movement to the rear of Washington's right wing, and inflicted on it and him crushing disaster. Long Island was full of forage, which afterwards was either destroyed or fed the horses of the British cavalry and artillery. So shockingly deficient was the American mounted service that on the very day when Clinton turned the American flank, Heath, the acting quartermaster-general of the patriot army, was writing from King's Bridge, a few miles away on Manhattan Island, to Mifflin, who was about to cross his command over the East River to Brooklyn, "We have not a single horse here. I have written to the General [Washington] for two or three." To a military critic, the attempt to hold the outer Long Island line under such circumstances seems little short of ineptitude.

General Sullivan, who was in command of that line, and who, together with Stirling, his next in command, was captured when his flank was turned, afterward claimed that he had all along felt uneasy about the Bedford road—that by which Howe effected his turning movement— and "had paid horsemen fifty dollars for patrolling [it] by night, while I had command, as I had no foot for the purpose." The plain inference would seem to be that none of the American commanders, from Washington down, had at this stage of the war any understanding of the use and absolute necessity of mounted men in field operations. A cavalry patrol fifty strong only, on the flank of the American advanced line on Brooklyn's right front, and patrolling the approaches, might, and probably would, by giving timely notice, have saved the commands of Sullivan and Stirling from the disaster of August twenty-seventh, and yet a few weeks before, the four hundred Connecticut mounted men had been sent home by Washington for the reason that cavalry could be of no service in military operations conducted "here, where horses cannot be brought into action." But, American or British, it was all of a piece; and the whole story of what occurred August 27 to 30, 1776, on Long Island, is on both sides suggestive only of a badly played game of chess, the result of which was that the losing party escaped a checkmate only through the quite unaccountable procrastination of his opponent on land, and the inactivity of that opponent on the water.

All this, as well as the subsequent transfer of the patriot army from Brooklyn across the East River to New York, occurred during the closing days of August. Four months later the affairs at Trenton and Princeton closed the campaign of 1776, and Washington's army went into its winter quarters at Morristown.

For present purposes, it is not necessary to review the incidents of that melancholy campaign or its redeeming, brilliant close in the Christmas week of 1776. It is sufficient to say that throughout those operations, from the ignominious Kip's Bay panic on September fifteenth to the splendid closing rally at Princeton on New Year's Day, 1777, there is nowhere any indication of the presence of mounted men connected with the patriot army, much less of any organized auxiliary cavalry service. Nor is it easy to see how the necessary courier and orderly work was done. Of patrol work, picket duty, and scouting service there was no pretense on either side. Indeed, it was to this fact, and the neglect on the part of the British of the most ordinary military precautions against surprise, that Washington owed his success at both Trenton and Princeton. Yet the second year of active operations was drawing to a close; and, certainly, operations during the last four months of that second year were not conducted "where horses" could not "be brought into action."

If Washington, in his Morristown winter quarters, subjected himself, as he doubtless did, to a rigid introspection, the first and most necessary requirement of the situation which suggested itself to him, ought to have been the creation of an adequate mounted force of some kind, attached to his command, at once his army's eyes and ears, its safeguard against surprise and his most ready weapon of offence.

And, as respects safeguard against surprise, Major-General Charles Lee, then second in command in the patriot army, furnished at this juncture and in his own person a most instructive illustration—though somewhat ludicrous as well. Howe had sent out Colonel Harcourt with a detachment apparently of the Seventeenth Light Dragoons to obtain information as to Lee's movements. This detachment seems to have roamed about, and finally Colonel Harcourt not only learned of General Lee's whereabouts, but also got full information as to how he was accompanied through an intercepted letter of Lee's, the delivery of which, no mounted force being available for even courier service, had been entrusted to "a countryman." Lee had gone out in order to reconnoiter, and stopped at a tavern. Lee had then foolishly taken up his quarters at the house in question, and had there slept. On the morning of the thirteenth of December, a fortnight to a day before the battle at Trenton, a mere squad of British cavalry, only thirty strong, swooped down on White's Tavern, near Baskingridge—halfway across the State of New Jersey—and in leisurely fashion, carried Lee off in slippers and dressing gown, a prisoner of war. Another point of interest in connection with this somewhat *opera bouffe* performance was the presence in it, as commander of the squadron, of Banastre Tarleton, then a cornet of light-horse—this was the Tarleton who subsequently gained so great notoriety as an active and enterprising cavalry officer in the Southern Department.

The capture of Charles Lee does, however, make clear that Howe's army in this campaign did boast a small force of regular cavalry, designated Light dragoons or Light-horse, and though it was mentioned from time to time, its only notable performance was this bagging of Charles Lee. None the less, it is apparent that, with a sufficient and effective auxiliary mounted force, such as Tarleton subsequently had under him in the Carolinas, the advantages gained in the operations about New York and New Jersey during the autumn months of 1776 by Howe and Cornwallis might easily have been followed up, and Washington's straggling and demoralized army might have been effectually dispersed. On the other hand, the British, from the lack of a mounted force adapted to irregular service and American conditions, did not follow up their successes. The Americans, for the same reason, were wholly unable to harass their enemy and retard his advance. They could not even keep informed as to that enemy's position and movements, much less cut off his supplies, or exhaust and distract him by continually beating up his cantonments—a system of tactics subsequently most successfully employed in the Carolina campaigns under even less advantageous conditions. During the earlier stages of that seven years' revolutionary struggle, the British failed to "catch on" so to speak, to this feature of warfare. However, the curious and hardly explicable fact, is that later, they did "catch on," and more quickly than Washington, who was to the manner born. But even with material directly at hand in the way of both horses and riders, it is a matter of wonder that no American Mosby developed anywhere or at any time within the field of operations presided over by Washington.

Further south, the partisan leader and the mounted rifleman appeared, as if by spontaneous generation. But north of the Chesapeake, where the initiative and personal influence of Washington set the gait—so to speak—any trace of this aggressive individual enterprise by mounted troops is absent. The men were there, the horses were there, forage was there, all in abundance. Only the organization and leaders were lacking. Nor were the leaders far to seek. Daniel Morgan, of Virginia, was there, Jersey-born, but of Welsh stock, no less a born commander of irregular horse than, eighty years later in the War of Secession was Forrest, of Tennessee, a man of exactly similar type, instinctively a strategist and cavalry leader.

To the military critic, Washington is something of a puzzle; for though ordinarily cautious and even slow, he was at times wonderfully alert, and at other times actually audacious. In the operations in and about New York during the autumn of 1776 he failed to grasp the strategic situation, and vacillated in presence of his opponent in a way which should have led to his destruction. The decision, alertness and energy displayed by him at Princeton and Trenton, and in the following year at Brandywine and Germantown where Washington challenged an opposing force which in organization and equipment completely outclassed his own, was simply confounding. When it came to the organization of a mounted force and its effective use in his operations, Washington did not evince mental alertness.

Campaign of 1777

The campaign of 1777—Washington's third—was marked by Burgoyne's invasion from Canada, and the ill-considered and altogether aimless movement of Sir William Howe on Philadelphia. The northern campaign began in the middle of June, and closed with the Saratoga surrender on the seventeenth of October. Burgoyne was a cavalry officer, and had won such distinction as he enjoyed by organizing the so-called "light-horse" as an arm of the English military service. Now, however, he was called upon to conduct operations in a nearly primeval wilderness, through which he should have moved by water whenever it was possible to do so, but elected instead to march by land.

Accordingly, the British and German soldiers, accustomed to European roads, found themselves following woodland trails through a country intersected by creeks, and consisting in great part of impassable morasses. Under such conditions, a mounted force would have been simply an additional encumbrance. Thus, in the Saratoga campaign, cavalry could cut no figure. But if there was no obvious use to be made of cavalry, or rather of an improvised force of mounted rangers, in the swampy wilderness at the head of Lake George and around Saratoga, it was quite otherwise in Maryland and southern and eastern Pennsylvania, the region which Howe selected as the field for his operations.

During the earlier months of that summer, there had been some desultory movements on the part of Howe, from New York as a base, which Washington had contented himself with observing. He was at this juncture pursuing a true Fabian policy. He was wise in so doing; for, in every branch of the service—infantry, artillery, even cavalry—the force opposed to him was incomparably superior to anything he could put into the field. At the time these operations were referred to in England as Howe's "two weeks fooling in New Jersey." It is surely needless to point out how valuable any mounted force, regular or irregular, would have been to the patriot commander while these operations were in process. Indeed, it is not easy to see how, without such an arm in his service, he managed to keep the field. His opponent must have been singularly devoid of anything even remotely resembling aggressive alertness. Presently Howe moved his army back to Staten Island, and loading it on transports, disappeared from view until the last days of July, when he turned up, so to speak, at the entrance of Delaware Bay.

Washington at once hurried his ill-organized command to the new field of operations. On his way, he passed through Philadelphia, where the Continental Congress was then sitting. From a letter written by John Adams to his wife, we get a glimpse of a more or less nebulous cavalry contingent as a component part of the patriot army. John Adams wrote: "Four regiments of light-horse, Bland's, Baylor's, Sheldon's, and Moylan's, four grand divisions of the army, and the artillery. They marched twelve deep, and yet took above two hours in passing by. General Washington and the other general officers with their aides on horseback. The Colonels and other field-officers on horseback."

No mention is in this letter made of the First Troop, Philadelphia City Cavalry, though that body acted as Washington's escort when he passed through the city.

Those in command apparently had no conception of an organized cavalry force, operating as such and as an independent unit. The service rendered by the Troop was for no particular or extended term, and consisted chiefly of courier duty, attendance at headquarters, and somewhat ineffective scouting, generally by individuals or small details.

Presently the British expedition made its appearance in Chesapeake Bay; and finally, a landing was effected near Elkton. Philadelphia—it was plain—was now the British objective, and Washington proceeded to plant himself in Howe's path. This was distinctly audacious, because he commanded a force some eleven thousand strong, only half-disciplined and wretchedly equipped, while Howe had eighteen thousand regulars, with an artillery contingent. Having arrived by sea, Howe could not have had any considerable force of mounted men, probably only a squadron or two.

What now ensued most strikingly illustrated the absence of cavalry on either side. To one trained practically in the methods of modern warfare it reads like a burlesque, exciting a sense of humor as well as a feeling of amazement. While Howe's army lay at Elkton, preparing in a leisurely way to take up its line of march to Philadelphia, Washington, it is said, accompanied by Greene and Lafayette, with a few aides, went forward to reconnoiter. In other words, the two generals, most prominent in the army and necessary to its preservation as well as effectiveness, accompanied by a distinguished foreign guest, actually went out in person on a scout. Riding forward to certain elevations, from which they got a glimpse of a few tents in the distance, Washington and his companions were caught on their return in a heavy rain, and took shelter for the night in a farmhouse that chanced to be owned and occupied by a loyalist. They seem to have been without escort and ran as great a risk of being gobbled up as Lee had, eight months before.

Judging by Lafayette's long subsequent account of this performance, Washington's companions passed some anxious hours that night.

It next devolved upon the patriot army to cover Philadelphia. Howe had a good idea as to the composition of the force opposed to him, the inadequacy of its equipment, its lack of cavalry or any mounted service, and its consequent inability to secure early and correct information as to his own whereabouts and tactics. He acted accordingly, preparing a flank movement almost exactly similar to that so successfully employed on Long Island the previous year. The lesson administered by Clinton at Flatbush on Long Island, had it would appear, not been sufficiently taken to heart. So, Cornwallis proceeded to administer it again at Birmingham meetinghouse, on the Brandywine. The complete absence of any effective mounted force was once more apparent, as well as the utter impracticability of successfully conducting military operations in a fairly open country without the assistance of cavalry.

Cornwallis, in immediate command of one of the two divisions into which Howe had, for this occasion, divided his army, proceeded to move around Washington's unsuspecting right. The reports which then reached General Washington were confused and contradictory. He had not the means of getting at the positive truth, because he was so weak in cavalry; and so the morning wore away amidst distracting doubts and varying counsels. Presently, as the result of a reconnaissance made by a single horseman sent out to explore by Sullivan, who commanded the American right, Washington was erroneously advised as to his opponent's probable plan of operations, and set his forces in motion for an attack on that portion of Howe's army in his own immediate front. Other and more correct information then at last reaching him, he again changed his plan, but it was then too late. Howe's flanking movement had been completely and successfully carried out. The disaster which a few hours later overwhelmed the patriot cause was due to the fact that those in charge of it could obtain no reliable information from the inhabitants, and had so few and insufficient cavalry that they could make no extended and rapid explorations. A year almost to a day had elapsed since this same Sullivan had found himself the victim of a precisely similar movement on Long Island, his opponent getting in his rear by a perfectly obvious roundabout route, but one over which an enemy's approach was never "dreamed of."

But now the absence of any cavalry contingent in Howe's army became equally apparent. An effective mounted force, energetically led, if then flung on Washington's disordered and retreating troops, could hardly have failed to convert the rout into a panic; and Washington might now have undergone the same experience at the hands of Cornwallis which Gates almost exactly three years later underwent at his and Tarleton's hands at Camden.

Washington owed his salvation to the absence of a British cavalry contingent, combined perhaps with the constitutional inertness of an opponent who never saw any occasion for following up an advantage. Having won what could easily have been made a decisive victory, Sir William Howe showed no disposition to assume an active pursuit, but lay for two weeks in camp in a healthy position on high ground, within a few miles of his successful battlefield.

During this inexplicable interval in active operations, the absence on the patriot side of any eyes and ears of an army received further forcible illustration in the so-called "Paoli Massacre" of September 20, through which "Mad Anthony" Wayne got a rough lesson in warfare. After the disaster on the Brandywine, when Washington withdrew across the Schuylkill, he left a small force, some fifteen hundred strong, on its further side, under Wayne, to watch Howe, and it is said to "harass his rear" if he moved forward. The reason given for such a risky division of a force, is not intelligible, and certainly infantry was here left to do what was plainly the work of cavalry. Wayne also was—like Sullivan on the Brandywine—without the means of effective outpost service. Apparently, he had a few very inefficient mounted men posted as videttes, who failed to give timely notice of the enemy's approach.

The natural result, a night surprise, followed. At about one o'clock in the morning, Wayne's camp was rushed, and he lost about a fifth of his command—lives thrown away.

During the previous winter Congress, presumably on the suggestion of Washington, had given some more or less shadowy consideration to the idea of organizing a body of what was termed "light cavalry," in apparent distinction to the thoroughly drilled and heavily accoutered dragoon. In Europe, the dragoon constituted the more solid mounted arm of the service, equipped with carbines, while the hussar and lancer, lighter and more dashing, depended on the saber and lance. Both were quite unfitted to the essential, but little understood, conditions of practical warfare in America.

It so chanced that Casimir Pulaski was the first Chief of Cavalry in the army of the United States. Commissioned by Congress a brigadier-general, September 13, 1777, he was afterwards assigned by Washington to the general command of what composed the mounted force of the patriot army; at that time, though the war was then far advanced in its third year of active operations, a quite inchoate branch of the service. It thus devolved on a Pole and an exile to make the first serious attempt to give form to a systematic American cavalry organization for actual use in practical warfare.

During the winter of 1776–1777 Congress once more authorized the formation of a mounted force; but whether any such force ever really came into existence, even on paper, is questionable. The historians make no mention of it. Meanwhile, Count Pulaski had now been for some time in the country and attached to Washington's headquarters as a member of his military family.

A showy, dashing Polish horseman, and as the end showed, a most generous and gallant young fellow, Pulaski, as Chief of Cavalry for the Continental army of 1778, labored under difficulties which were in fact insuperable. With a quick temper and impatient disposition, he could not make himself understood in English, and a stranger in a strange land, his whole former military experience was, among Americans and under American conditions, a positive drawback. He submitted a sensible memorandum to Washington in which he pointed out clearly the pressing necessity of an organized and improved cavalry service; and subsequently, he forwarded several reports setting forth in most imperfect English the difficulties he encountered.

But while Pulaski addressed himself with zeal to the task assigned him, he plainly did not go at it in the right way—in the way in which, for instance, Morgan would probably have gone at it. In other words, he did not understand America, and had no correct idea as to conditions. Consequently, the officers of the several regiments, who had heretofore been in a measure independent, were not easily reconciled to the orders of a superior, particularly of a foreigner who did not understand their language, and whose ideas of discipline, arrangement, and maneuvers were different from those to which they had been accustomed. The result naturally to be expected in due time ensued. Thus, the first attempt at a Continental cavalry organization failed. It failed because it was in no way American, or entered upon with a correct appreciation of existing potentialities. And so, the brave and unfortunate Pulaski passed on to his early death. It was merely another case of a square peg in a round hole. But the question still presents itself—who put the peg in that particular hole?—and did the person making the assignment [Washington] exactly understand either the nature of the hole or the adaptation of the peg to it?

And this query leads to the very heart of the historical topic now under consideration. Stated broadly and as an abstract military proposition, there is no branch of the service in which a familiar acquaintance with the country to be operated in, and its conditions, is so essential to a commander's success, as in the cavalry.

And after two whole years of campaigning in the Jerseys and Pennsylvania, Washington, it might not unreasonably be assumed, should have grasped this elementary proposition. That he did so grasp it, there is no evidence whether in his operations or his correspondence. Yet the third year of active warfare was now drawing to its end, and while poor Pulaski was struggling in vain with the English language and a "Legion" cavalry organization at once ill-considered and insubordinate, both Morgan and Arnold were in command of men who ought to have been on horseback with rifles on their saddlebows, but who still marched and fought on foot with musket and bayonet.

To return, however, to the Brandywine and the course of military events. The battle was fought September 11, and toward the close of that month, Howe skillfully outmaneuvered Washington, threw his army across the Schuylkill, and occupied Philadelphia. This has been pronounced "the cleverest piece of work" ever accomplished by him, but his success in it was again entirely due to Washington's absolute lack of any approach to an effective outpost service.

The battle of Germantown followed, involving of course, the continued occupation of Philadelphia by the British. An audacious conception, and well planned, it came near being a brilliant success. Unfortunately, there was no possibility of quick communication on the field; owing to the prevalence of dense fog, the position of the enemy could not be correctly ascertained, and the small mounted force available, amounting in all perhaps to some four hundred men, was divided up among the several commands for headquarter and orderly service. But, considering the nature of the locality, and the atmospheric conditions which that morning prevailed, it is at least questionable whether at Germantown any opportunity presented itself for the effective use of horse. The force there present, referred to in the accounts of the affair as "Pulaski's cavalry," is the first recognition of the mounted man as a distinctive branch of American army organization.

Such was the close of the campaign of 1777. Valley Forge followed. On the nineteenth of December, Washington led his now wholly demoralized following, an army in name only, along the western bank of the Schuylkill to their doleful winter quarters at Valley Forge.

Summarizing the campaign of 1777, so far as the operations conducted by Washington in person were concerned, one historian says that if Washington had "begun the campaign with a respectable force of cavalry, numerous enough to cover his own front and watch the movements of the enemy, his advance guard need never have been surprised at Paoli, and even Brandywine might have told another tale." He then adds that Washington, during the Valley Forge winter, gave much of both time and thought to the creation of such a force. The organization of what was subsequently known as "Lee's Legion" resulted. Though doubtless Washington gave closest attention to everything which concerned the enlistment, the equipment, and above all, the mounting of the troopers composing this body, yet that very corps, famous as it subsequently became in Revolutionary annals, and brilliant and effective as the work done by it unquestionably was, emphasizes forcibly Washington's limitations as a cavalry leader, and his failure to grasp in a large way the part which a sufficient and effective mounted service, both might and should have played in the general field of operations.

Why was this so? "Lee's Legion," modeled, by the way, on Pulaski's ill-conceived idea of an effective American cavalry service, consisted of some three hundred men, one-half only of whom were mounted. Instead of organizing a cavalry command of such wholly inadequate proportions, why was King's Mountain not anticipated, and a call sent out for the frontiersmen and rangers of Virginia and Pennsylvania to come riding in on their own horses? Why were not Morgan's riflemen jerked into the saddle, where they would have felt far more at home than on their feet?

The explanation seems obvious. Washington began his military career as a backwoods Indian fighter, and he never forgot the lessons then learned, nor outgrew that experience. In the wooded wildernesses of the Alleghenies cavalry could not operate. And so, Virginian though he was, from the beginning to the end of his military life, there is so far as can be discovered, no indication of any adequate conception of the value and importance of the mounted man in military operations, and more especially in that particular form of military operation which it devolved upon him to conduct. Yet it is the first business of any great soldier both to appreciate and study the nature of the weapons at his command, and then to make full and effective use of them.

Campaign of 1778

If this limitation of Washington's military capacity was obvious in the two campaigns of 1776 and 1777 that of 1778 emphasized the deficiency. The campaign opened, inauspiciously enough, with the somewhat inexplicable Barren Hill performance, under the leadership of a boy of twenty. Lafayette at that time still lacked six months of attaining his majority. Though May was well advanced, active operations had not yet begun. The British army, still under the command of Sir William Howe—though, being superseded by Clinton, he was about to sail for England—occupied Philadelphia, while the patriots, just again gathering strength after their terrible winter experience, remained at Valley Forge. Washington determined to feel the enemy, and with that end in view, sent out a detachment, some fifteen hundred strong, of his best troops, with Lafayette in command. It was, in fact, a reconnaissance in force, and as such, should have been composed in the main of cavalry, with a strong infantry support and artillery contingent. The patriot army, however, had no cavalry to speak of, so Lafayette marched off with a command composed almost exclusively of foot. Crossing the Schuylkill by a ford some two hours' march from Valley Forge, he advanced to Barren Hill, within twelve miles of Philadelphia, and there went into camp. What ensued illustrates especially, the extreme danger of attempting a close reconnaissance of an enemy of superior force without cavalry. The British were fully informed as to his movement and arranged to bag Lafayette and his command. By merest chance, and combined with the dull incompetence of Major-General Grant, who commanded one of the British columns, the bagging plan failed by the narrowest of margins. But it is instructive, and the whole episode affords an interesting example both of the absence and misuse of the weapons essential to success in warfare. However, Washington did profit by the experience, for he was careful to risk no more valuable detachments to watch for the evacuation of Philadelphia. In other words, having no cavalry to send, he sent out no more infantry to do cavalry work.

All this was preliminary, and it was not until a month later on June 18 that the campaign really opened. During that month Washington was observing Clinton closely, knowing full well that the British army must move, but in doubt as to the direction of that movement. It would seem that the utmost mobility on his own part should have been his first concern. June 1778 witnessed at last the withdrawal of the British army from Philadelphia, and its inglorious, but successful, transfer across New Jersey to New York. Its escape from total destruction was then largely due to the absence of cavalry as a factor of efficiency in the patriot army. Why, at this advanced stage of the war, it should have been lacking is not apparent. When Clinton set out on his march from Philadelphia to New York, his army had at its disposition no less than five thousand horses, almost all of which had been collected by requisition or purchase during Sir William Howe's occupation of Pennsylvania. General Greene, Washington's quartermaster, had secured a vast quantity of horses for the artillery and transport of the patriot army during the same period. Pennsylvania as well as Virginia was well supplied with mounts, and with Virginia only the other side of the Potomac, troopers would naturally not have been far to seek.

Sir Henry Clinton had now succeeded Sir William Howe. For good and sufficient reasons, when his position at Philadelphia had become difficult as well as objectless, he decided to transfer himself to New York. It was in fact a withdrawal from a position no longer tena-

ble. For equally satisfying reasons, it was determined to make the transfer by a land march. When the British army started on its return, the
movement was not unanticipated on the part of Washington; and it is
curious in reading the narratives to note through incidental mentions
how very gradually it was that the use of mounted men, in the kind
of warfare they were then engaged in, dawned on the patriot leaders.
While, for instance, Clinton's troops passed out of Philadelphia and
crossed the river at dawn, six hours later a part of Major "Light Horse
Harry" Lee's dragoons galloped down to the quay just in time to see the
English rear guard off, as it ferried across the Delaware.

One thing however is undeniable. No military movement could
possibly have been much more open to fatal disaster through an application of Parthian [hit-and-run] tactics than that march of the British
army from Philadelphia to Sandy Hook, in June 1778. When the British
reached their second halting-place, the rain poured down for fourteen
consecutive hours, ruining the highways, soaking the baggage, spoiling
the ammunition and provisions, and drenching the soldiers to the skin.
Under these conditions Clinton's progress was inordinately slow, and
he consumed a full week over the first forty miles of his journey. The
heat then became intense, and the British infantry, burdened like pack
horses, were preceded by a train of carts a dozen miles in length and
frequently compelled to travel on a single road. The whole countryside
was up in arms, bent on impeding his progress, and Sir Henry Clinton
had no cavalry. All the bridges over which the column had to pass were
broken down. The road, such as it was, "was execrable, and the heat like
the desert of Sahara." When the retreating army got in motion, on the
torrid morning of the eleventh day, "innumerable carriages gradually
wound themselves out of the meadows where they had been parked,
and covered in unbroken file the whole of the eleven miles of highway
which led northward from Monmouth Court House to the village of
Middletown." It was here that the American infantry, under General
Charles Lee, struck the retreating column.

Since Washington's unhappy experience on Long Island in August 1776, he had struggled through nearly two entire years of campaign work, at once active and disastrous. But now Charles Lee found himself, as respects mounted men and field intelligence, in almost exactly the position of Sullivan before Brooklyn and on the Brandywine. It seems incredible, but so wholly without cavalry was the general in charge of Washington's leading division in the advance to Monmouth, that at seven o'clock on the evening before the battle, unable to get any precise information as to his enemies' whereabouts, Lee hurriedly wrote to Washington that "the people here are inconceivably stupid. I have sent two lively young footmen, for they have no horses, to reconnoiter." Then he added in a postscript, "I wish your Excellency would order me two or three, if they can be spared, active, well-mounted, light-horsemen."

It is curious to reflect on what might, under the general conditions of time, place, season, topography and movement, have been the result had the Americans at this stage of the war resorted to Parthian tactics. But the military as well as historic truth is that, on this as on other occasions, Washington measured himself and his army up against his adversary at the point where they were strongest and he was least so. He opposed infantry to infantry, oblivious of the fact that the British infantry were of the most perfectly organized kind, while his own was at best an extemporized force. The natural result followed. Whatever the mounted force under Harry Lee or Allan McLane may have been, it is apparent that it was not sufficient to cut any figure during the momentous movement culminating at Monmouth Court House. To a wagon train, eleven miles in length, the American cavalry offered no disturbing obstacle. To have stopped that train's forward movement, and in so doing, to have thrown the whole column into confusion, would have been a simple matter. But the weapon was not at hand. It was by a margin of only five days that Clinton's army escaped disaster, if not total destruction.

Drawing inferences from this record, would it be unfair to conclude that two thousand of the King's Mountain rangers, led say, by Daniel Morgan, might during those ten days of transfer, have very potently contributed towards then and there ending the War of Independence?

No more pitched battles were fought in the North. Washington never again met Clinton in the field. The two commanders, one impregnably entrenched in the Highlands along the Hudson River, and the other impregnably entrenched in the town of New York, simply watched each other, from July 1778, until September 1781, when Washington made his sudden move to Yorktown, Virginia.

Campaigns of 1779–1781

After Monmouth, the seat of active Revolutionary warfare was transferred from the vicinity of New York and the Jerseys to the Carolinas, and General Nathanael Greene, in place of Washington, directed operations. Before Greene superseded Gates, one incident connected with the latter's southern fiasco is suggestive in the present connection. When Gates first assumed command in the South, some of the officers with experience in his new Department, especially Colonel White and Lieutenant-Colonel Washington, both of whom had commanded mounted men, pressed on his attention the importance of that branch of the service in the country in which he now had to operate. Gates paid no attention to their suggestions. His indifference probably resulted from his experience at Saratoga where, as already pointed out, cavalry could, from the nature of the country and the conditions under which operations were conducted, perform no obviously important service. In his memoirs, "Light Horse Harry" Lee attributes the neglect of their advice as the reason for the crushing disaster which befell Gates at Camden. "In no country in the world," Lee adds, "were the services of the cavalry more to be desired than was that which was committed to Major-General Gates, and how it was possible for an officer of his experience to have been regardless of this powerful auxiliary remains inexplicable."

It is not necessary here to enter in detail into the operations conducted in the Carolinas between the occupation of Charleston by the British, in May 1780, and their final evacuation of South Carolina in September 1782. It is sufficient to say that, as a military study, from the cavalry point of view, those operations afford a striking contrast to what had previously taken place during an almost exactly similar space of time in the Northern Department.

There was, it is true, a large royalist faction in the Carolinas, but the same element was found in almost equal proportion in New York, New Jersey and Pennsylvania. The horse was equally at hand in each region, while forage was more plentiful in the northern than in the southern states. But it seemed as though both sides—American and British, simultaneously and as if from instinct—"caught on" in the Carolinas. For instance, Savannah surrendered to the British on the eleventh of May 1780, and by the twenty-ninth of the same month, only eighteen days later, Tarleton had behind him seven hundred mounted men when he surprised Colonel Buford at the Waxhaws and nearly destroyed his entire command. The British officer had covered one hundred and fifty-four miles in fifty-four hours. This was great cavalry work. Nothing like it was attempted, much less accomplished, by any of Washington's command in the Monmouth campaign.

The tactics employed on both sides in the Carolina struggle were largely partisan. Irregular bodies, the men mounted on their own horses, called together at a moment's notice and separating at the will of those composing the band, harried the countryside, cut off detached parties, showed small mercy to prisoners, and withal, did little in the way of effective work towards bringing the war to an end. Rather it was a process of exhaustion.

The one cause for wonder is, how Greene, without arms, munitions, clothing, commissariat or camp-chest, contrived to keep the field at all. As to Greene, it is impossible now to say whether he possessed in any marked degree the elements of an officer of cavalry. He did however fully realize, as a result of experience, the immense importance of that arm of the service, causing him to write to Lafayette, when the latter was conducting operations in Virginia, the enemy "are increasing their cavalry by every means in their power, and have a greater number than we have, though not of equal goodness. We are trying to increase ours. Enlarge your cavalry or you are inevitably ruined."

It is a curious and very noticeable fact also, that as respects both the organization of cavalry and its effective use, the British not only seem to have taken the initiative, but they held their advantage up to the close of the struggle. In other words, while cavalry in the southern campaigns of Cornwallis acted as an adjunct in military operations and was used effectively in this way, this on the patriot side was the case only to a very limited extent. The only cavalry Greene could depend upon as an effective weapon in his immediate command, were the comparatively insignificant organizations commanded by Harry Lee and Lieutenant-Colonel William Washington. On the other hand, Pickens, Marion, Sumter and the rest gave Greene almost as much trouble as they rendered him assistance. He was continually making futile attempts to draw them under his personal control for some concentrated movement; while they, much older men, natives of the country, and plainly more or less jealous of his, the Rhode Islander's, authority, acted on their own responsibility, obeying or neglecting to obey his orders much as they saw fit.

Two conflicts, however, which occurred in the Carolinas, the one at King's Mountain on October 6, 1780, the other at the Cowpens on January 17, 1781, are especially noteworthy.

At King's Mountain the whole patriot force—less than fourteen hundred "over-mountain men" as they were called—suddenly concentrated, having covered a considerable distance with great rapidity. As soon as they arrived near the base of the spur [on which the conflict occurred] the riflemen all dismounted and, leaving their coats and blankets strapped to the saddles, tied their horses in the woods and with scarcely a moment's delay started on foot up the three easy sides of the spur. The account of this episode is curiously suggestive. These men, the wild and fierce inhabitants of Kentucky, and other settlements west of the Allegheny Mountains were all well mounted on horseback and armed with rifles. Each carried his own provisions in a wallet, so that no encumbrance of wagons, or delays of commissary departments, impeded their movements.

Three months later, at Cowpens (January 17, 1781), Daniel Morgan gave evidence of the possession of all the attributes of a born military commander and cavalry leader. Making his dispositions without regard for accepted military rules, he availed himself in the best way possible of the weapons at his command. He had a small force of cavalry only, amounting perhaps to one hundred and fifty troopers. They were under the command of William Washington; and these he flung upon Tarleton's flank at the crisis of the action, in a manner so effective that the British defeat became at once a rout. One of the very few outright patriot victories of the entire war, Cowpens was altogether the most neatly, though unscientifically, fought battle of the war.

While Greene's operations were most skillfully and persistently conducted, they indicated the attributes of an excellent commander of infantry, rather than the dashing qualities of one either accustomed to the handling of cavalry or naturally inclined to it. Both Guilford Court House and Eutaw Springs could have been turned from defeats, or at best indecisive actions, into complete victories, had Greene then had an effective force of cavalry, and like Morgan, known exactly when and how to make use of it. Even as it was, his small body of mounted men, under command of Lee and Washington, rendered effective service on more than one occasion. As to the notorious Tarleton, he proved the right arm, such as it was, of Cornwallis, and the raids led by him, both in the Carolinas and in Virginia, though they seem extraordinary in dash and daring, contributed little to an effective prosecution of the war against the Americans.

Mounted Troops of the Mexican War

During the Mexican War, the United States mounted units consisted of two types of troops. The first of these were the "Dragoons," who were armed with musketoons, which they carried on sling belts. They also carried sabers of the straight Prussian pattern, and horse pistols. The second type of horse warriors were the "Mounted Rifles." They were armed with percussion rifles and horse pistols, and though sabers were reserved for officers only, most troopers carried large Bowie knives the size of short swords.

The following sections are adapted from the History of the United States Cavalry *by Albert G. Brackett.*

Thornton Captured

In the year 1845, Brevet Brigadier General Zachary Taylor had assembled quite a respectable United States force at Corpus Christi, on the coast of Texas, and early in the spring of 1846 moved to the Rio Grande, and threw up a field work, which has since been known as Fort Brown, on the banks of that stream. Arista, the Mexican commander, hearing of this, sent a force of twenty-five hundred men, under General

Torrejon, to the Texas side of the Rio Grande, with a view of commencing hostilities against the Americans, and plainly stated such to be his intention to General Taylor. The latter sent Captain Thornton, with a squadron of the 2nd Dragoons, to watch his movements. He proceeded about sixteen miles above the fort, when his guide refused to go farther; but Thornton, wishing to carry out the full instructions of Taylor, and learn as much as possible about the enemy, whom he believed had not yet crossed from the Mexican side of the river, continued on. He moved about three miles farther, when, halting near a ranch, he sent his men inside of an enclosure, or corral, to feed their horses, and soon followed himself. The Mexicans were discovered at the farther end, when the dragoons attempted to get outside, but found the entrance closed on them. Thornton was severely wounded, and his horse was shot out from under him by the first fire of the Mexicans. After a sharp fire, which the dragoons were unable to return with effect, as the Mexicans were outside the pickets of the enclosure, Captain Hardee, who took command on the fall of Thornton, surrendered. This occurred on April 24, 1846.

Mason Killed

Second Lieutenant George T. Mason was killed in this affair, and sixteen dragoons were killed and wounded. The prisoners were taken to Matamoros, and were subsequently exchanged. This seemed an unfavorable commencement of hostilities, and had a dispiriting influence on the army, and General Taylor himself was considerably annoyed by it.

Palo Alto

The fort was completed, and Taylor, leaving a sufficient force to guard it, started for Point Isabel to obtain supplies and then return. He took with him the greater part of his army, as the Mexicans had by this time crossed the Rio Grande in large numbers, and a battle was considered imminent. Taylor obtained his supplies, and started on his return to

Fort Brown on May 7, having with him a train of three hundred wagons. On May 8, the battle of Palo Alto was fought. In this action Captain Croghan Ker's squadron of the Second Dragoons guarded the train, and the colonel of that regiment (Twiggs) acted as brigadier general commanding one of the wings of the American army.

May's Charge at Resaca de la Palma

Sending his wounded to Point Isabel, and leaving his train with a sufficient guard at Palo Alto, Taylor moved forward with his army, and came up with the Mexican force at a place known as Resaca de la Palma. Here he found it necessary to attack the enemy under most disadvantageous circumstances, but knowing it would not do to falter, he sent his troops forward, and the action commenced. A deep ravine separated the two armies, which was defended on the Mexican side by a number of pieces of artillery, which kept up a heavy firing upon the Americans as they advanced. The American infantry was broken up into small parties trying to force the passage of the ravine, when Taylor ordered Captain Charles A. May's squadron of the Second Dragoons forward to charge a battery which annoyed our people excessively. May's squadron consisted of his own and Lawrence Pike Graham's companies, and moved forward down the road at a gallop, and pulling up for a moment when near Ridgely's battery of artillery, the latter poured a heavy fire into the Mexicans, and May went thundering forward with the dragoons under cover of the smoke. On they went among the Mexicans, who, frightened by their impetuosity, broke in all directions, and their guns were captured. But in the melee, the dragoons were greatly scattered, and riding about furiously amid the smoke of battle. May, however, rallied a party, and, taking General La Vega prisoner, carried him off under a severe fire from the Mexican infantry. Ridgely had meanwhile galloped forward with his guns, and, halting for a short time for the dragoons to get out of the way, poured a terrible fire into the Mexicans, who had again formed near their guns. The Eighth Infantry and a portion of the Fifth came down the road at double-quick under Colonel Belknap, crossed the ravine, and the battle was won. Some parties kept up the firing some time longer, and the Mexicans gradually faded away in the distance.

This was a fine cavalry charge, but First Lieutenant Zebulon M. P. Inge was killed, as well as several dragoons, and quite a number were wounded. May was breveted lieutenant colonel for his conduct in this battle; Captain Graham was breveted major; First Lieutenants Ripley A. Arnold and Oscar F. Winship were breveted captains; and Second Lieutenants Alfred Pleasanton and Delos B. Sackett were breveted first lieutenants, all of them of the Second Dragoons. The fame of this charge added greatly to the reputation of the dragoons.

Rio Grande Crossed

After the battle Taylor's force continued its course toward the Rio Grande, and reached Fort Brown in safety. He prepared to cross that river, and by May 20 his whole force, except the garrison at Fort Brown and a small party at Point Isabel, was on the soil of Mexico. In crossing the river on the eighteenth of that month, Second Lieutenant George Stevens, Second Dragoons, an officer of promise, was drowned.

Taylor's army did not remain long at Matamoros, but gradually worked its way up the Rio Grande. While boats were brought from the United States, means of transportation accumulated before a forward movement was attempted. Twelve months volunteers were called for by the President. In response to this call, besides raising infantry, Kentucky sent one regiment of cavalry, Tennessee one, Missouri two, Arkansas one, Eastern Texas one, and Western Texas one.

Regiment of Mounted Riflemen Raised

On the May 19, 1846, another law was passed by Congress to provide for establishing military stations on the route to the Oregon territory, and to raise a regiment of mounted riflemen. This unit was accordingly raised, though it was not sent to Oregon, but upon its completion was sent to Mexico, where (with the exception of two companies which were eventually mounted) it did a great deal of good service as foot riflemen, the horses of the regiment having been lost by ship wreck in the Gulf of Mexico, and no opportunity occurring for obtaining remounts.

Colonel Persifer F. Smith, of Louisiana, was named colonel of this regiment. He was a lawyer of New Orleans, but had seen service as colonel of a regiment of Louisiana volunteers during the Florida War, and as brigadier general of a brigade of six regiments of Louisiana six months men, who first went to reinforce General Taylor. He was a good soldier, having given a great deal of attention to military affairs while a civilian; and soon after being appointed was placed in command of a brigade of regulars.

Brevet Captain John C. Fremont, of the Topographical Engineers was born in South Carolina, had seen considerable service, and was mainly known at that time on account of his explorations to and beyond the Rocky Mountains. At the time of his appointment he was among the mountains, and led a battalion of mounted California volunteers, mostly American mountaineers, in the conquest of California. He never served with his regiment.

Taylor at Monterey

General Taylor, after leaving suitable garrisons at different points on the Rio Grande, moved up that stream with a majority of his army to Camargo, and on August 19 set out for Monterey, where it was known a large force of Mexicans had assembled, and had fortified the town. By this time many of the volunteers had arrived from the North, and had been organized into a division under General Butler of Kentucky. The mounted force which accompanied the army consisted of four companies of the Second Dragoons, under Brevet Lieutenant Colonel May, who had distinguished himself at Palo Alto and at Resaca de la Palma; and Colonel Jack Hays's and Colonel Woods's regiments of Texans, or, as they were called, "Texas Rangers." These rangers were good troops for reconnaissance and for scouting, but were of little use for anything like regular movements. The march was not opposed, though parties of Mexican lancers were frequently seen on the road; but they did not interfere, having been thrown out by their own commander to watch our operations.

On the September 19, Taylor arrived in front of Monterey. This city, the capital of the State of Nuevo Leon, is situated on the little river San Juan, in the midst of a delightful plain, which is shut in on the west by lofty spurs of the Sierra Madre Mountains. Pure streams of fresh water trickle down the mountains, and in the irrigated bottom lands the finest crops can be raised without difficulty. It was at that time a town of about ten thousand inhabitants, and though far away on the frontier, possessed some fine buildings and a good-sized population. Ampudia, the Mexican commandant, had used every means in his power to strengthen the place, and had assured his own government that he was able to check the farther advance of the Americans into the interior. His force was made up of regular and irregular Mexican soldiers, and on the whole, was a very respectable army.

General Taylor arranged his plan of attack on the morning of the twentieth. General Worth, with his division, was ordered to move around to the right of the town through the cornfields, and gain, if possible, the Saltillo road above it, and thus cut off supplies and reinforcements which were expected to arrive for the Mexicans from the interior.

Twiggs's division was to attack in front, together with the volunteers under Butler. The mounted force which accompanied Worth in his detour to the right consisted of Hays's rangers; but Taylor, thinking this not strong enough, sent May's four companies of dragoons and Woods's regiment to reinforce him. The attack upon the town had by this time commenced, and the Mexicans returned fire in a most determined and spirited manner. Upon arriving in the vicinity of the Hill of Independence, on his way to join Worth, May found the fire of the guns upon its summit too hot for him, and halted out of range of them. General Henderson soon arrived with Woods's regiment, assumed command, and sent back to Taylor for instructions as to what he should do; but the cavalry arrived too late to be of any service.

Meanwhile Twiggs and Butler were working away at the city, and Worth was moving around. On the twenty-first, as Hays's regiment was passing a spur of the mountains, it came suddenly upon a Mexican regiment of Guanajuato lancers, supported by an infantry force. As soon as they were discovered, Hays halted his regiment, deployed, and moved down to a cornfield, where two companies were dismounted, and placed in ambush amid the thick bushes and fences of the field. One company pushed forward, fired, and returned toward the main body, drawing the lancers forward, who came on in fine style. The lancers galloped on, but were met by Smith's battalion of infantry, which was advancing in open order. The skirmishers opened a scattering fire, but the lancers, under Lieutenant Colonel Don Juan Najira, seemed not disposed to halt or give way. At this moment, however, the Texans, who were dismounted and concealed in the bushes, opened a most deadly fire upon them, when they turned, and tried to get back to the Saltillo road. Their efforts in this direction were foiled, when they attempted to cross over the hill, which was clear of our men, and presented their only chance of escape. But none succeeded, and the gallant young Colonel Najira, who refused to surrender although left alone, was struck by a bullet, and rolled off his horse dead. His behavior in this fight elicited the admiration of every one.

Soon the Mexican infantry fell back, and Worth pushed his men forward toward *La loma Federacion*. The fight above was the only cavalry engagement which occurred during the attack upon Monterey. The Texas troops dismounted, and fought their way into town on foot with the other troops.

After a bloody conflict of three days' duration, the Mexican force capitulated and surrendered the city to the Americans. During the morning of the twenty-fifth, the Mexican garrison evacuated the citadel, and on successive days the different corps left the town and marched to Saltillo. On the twenty-eighth, the last corps left the town and Worth occupied it with his division.

Cavalry Operations in California

While these events transpired in Northern Mexico, events of the most startling character, and which have been of the greatest importance, were being carried on in California, and on the plains between the Mississippi River and the Pacific. Captain Fremont, with a command made up of well-mounted mountaineers and backwoodsmen, had made his way beyond the Rocky Mountains, and had visited a portion of the Territory of Oregon; but with winter approaching, and he seeing no safe and secure place in which to pass it, pushed his way south, and in the month of January 1846, arrived within one hundred miles of Monterey, California, which is situated on the Pacific Ocean. As his animals needed rest, he decided to halt in the valley of the San Joaquin, which was filled with game, and which he had previously explored. Besides this, he found good water and abundance of grass, articles which he most stood in need of. To avoid trouble, he left his party in the valley of the San Joaquin, and proceeded in person to Monterey to visit General De Castro, the military *commandante*, where he explained his needs, and as his was an expedition of a purely peaceful character, he having been sent out in the first instance to make explorations of roads and routes leading from our Western settlements to the then far-off country of Oregon, De Castro, after some demur, finally gave his permission for the Americans to remain for a time, and Fremont left to join his little command of mounted men, thinking all was well, and that he would have no trouble. In this, however, he was mistaken. Scarcely had he left before De Castro sent out his messengers calling upon the people to rise and expel Fremont and his little band of Americans. After this news was transmitted to Fremont, he moved his command near to Monterey, and took a position on the San Juan Mountain, commonly called "Gavilan," from where he was able to overlook an immense extent of country, and here he unfurled the United States flag, determined to stand or fall in its defense. De Castro approached with his forces, but did not attack, and after remaining in a threatening attitude for several days, the Americans abandoned the mountain, and started for Oregon. De Castro followed with a force, which outnumbered Fremont's six times over, and continued to dog his trail for several days.

Finally, De Castro gave up the pursuit, and Fremont continued on his course, his progress north being impeded by natural obstacles, and by the hostility of the Tlamath Indians, who attacked him, and killed and wounded several of his men.

On May 9, he was overtaken by Lieutenant Gillespie, of the Marine Corps, who had made his way across the Republic of Mexico from Vera Cruz. From him he learned the condition of affairs in the States, and the likelihood of a war with Mexico. Determining, therefore, to return and face the danger which threatened him in rear, and to protect the American settlers who lived on the banks of the Rio de los Americanos, whom De Castro had proclaimed his intention of expelling from the country, he returned to the Bay of San Francisco with his party. The security of his own men, and of his countrymen living in California, made it necessary that measures should be taken at once, and after due deliberation, he decided to overthrow the Mexican authority in California.

Fremont commenced operations on June 11 by seizing a drove of two hundred horses, which was on its way to De Castro's camp in charge of an officer and fourteen men. He next attacked the military post of Sonoma, which was taken on the fifteenth of the same month, together with the garrison, consisting of General Vallejo, several officers and men, nine brass cannon, and two hundred fifty stand of arms. Leaving a small guard at Sonoma, Fremont set out for the Rio de los Americanos, where he recruited several volunteers from among the American settlers. Then hearing that De Castro intended to attack Sonoma during his absence, he returned, arriving on the morning of

June 25. He attacked the Mexicans under De la Torre, one of De Castro's subordinates, and defeated him near Sonoma.

Having succeeded in driving the Mexicans from the northern shore of the bay, Lieutenant Colonel Fremont (for he had been promoted, as before stated, as lieutenant colonel of the Mounted Rifle regiment) returned to Sonoma July 4. He called the Americans together, and, after explaining the state of affairs to them, a declaration of independence from Mexico was agreed upon, and Fremont was chosen as the director of affairs. De Castro meantime had established himself at Santa Clara, where he had entrenched himself on the south side of the bay, with two pieces of cannon and four hundred men. The Americans decided to attack him, and traveling one hundred miles in three days, reached the American settlements at the forks of the Sacramento. There they learned that De Castro had abandoned his works at Santa Clara, and retreated to the Cuidad de los Angeles on the Pacific, which was the place of residence of the governor general of the Californias, and about four hundred miles south of San Francisco. Everything was prepared for following De Castro, when news of the declaration of war between the United States and Mexico reached Fremont. He also learned that Commodore Sloat, who commanded the American squadron on the Pacific, had taken the several Mexican ports. Commodore Sloat, Commodore Stockton, and Lieutenant Colonel Fremont met at Monterey in July. Shortly thereafter Sloat, whose health was failing, returned to the United States. Stockton was left in command of the squadron, and cooperated heartily with Fremont. On July 25, Fremont's battalion was taken on board the United States ship *Cyane*, and started for the Cuidad de los Angeles, where Governor Pico and General De Castro had assembled a large Mexican force. Fremont's force was landed at San Diego, but there he found it difficult to procure a remount of horses.

However, after much labor, he succeeded, and then proceeded to join Stockton, who had landed at San Pedro, and was drilling his sailors and marines for duty on land. While these officers and men were preparing themselves for battle, Stockton received several messages from De Castro. To these he replied, telling him he would attack him as soon as he had prepared his forces. Stockton started for the Cuidad de los Angeles, and sent word to Fremont to join him en route. The Americans, as they neared that place, learned that the Mexican leaders had become frightened, and were on their way to the Mexican state of Sonora, which was farther south. Upon learning this, Stockton and Fremont entered the city on August 15, and on August 17 Stockton issued a proclamation announcing the conquest of California, and promising a government similar to that of the American Territories as soon as it could be established. Stockton announced himself as governor, and Lieutenant Colonel Fremont military commandant.

Kearney Invades New Mexico

In the meantime, Colonel Kearney had started from Fort Leavenworth with a force of eight companies of dragoons and some volunteers, intending the conquest of New Mexico. He was followed on his way by a band of Mormons, who were mustered into the service, and formed into a battalion under command of Lieutenant Colonel P. St. George Cooke, who was then a captain in the 1st Dragoons. Lieutenant Colonel James Allen, the first commander of this battalion, was also a captain in the 1st Dragoons, but died at Leavenworth on August 23, 1846. The regular dragoons were commanded by Sumner. Pursuing the military road to the westward, this "Army of the West" crossed the grassy prairies which lie between the Missouri and Kansas Rivers. On the Fourth of July they struck the main road leading from Independence to Santa Fe at Elm Grove, and were soon on the great plains, which extend for miles and miles in every direction, giving pasture-ground to the buffalo and elk. Occasionally they passed small watercourses, which wended their way toward the great "Father of Waters," and then upon the sandy plains, where the short, dry grass was interspersed with stunted bushes.

Trees were scarce, and only seen at long intervals. The army reached the Arkansas on the 19th of July, and continued its march along the northern bank to Bent's Fort, a small post erected by some citizens to serve as a trading post with the Indians. This served as the rendezvous for the different detachments, and here a large amount of provisions had previously been cached for Kearney's force.

Here Kearney rested his men, and supplied his artillery with mules, his horses having become completely broken down. He then pushed forward toward New Mexico. After leaving the valley of the Arkansas he came into a mountainous country. His road lay along the spurs of the Rocky Mountains, near the headwaters of the Cimarron and Canadian Rivers, and those of the Rio Grande.

Colonel Kearney reached Santa Fe on August 18 without any incident occurring worthy of note, and assumed control of affairs. He issued a proclamation declaring New Mexico to be a part of the United States, and absolving the inhabitants from their allegiance to the Mexican government, and claiming them as American citizens. A civil government was organized, and the proper officers appointed.

Kearney Moves on California

Afterwards Kearney set out for California on September 25, to assist in the conquest of that country. On October 5, 1846, he met an express from Commodore Stockton and Lieutenant Colonel Fremont reporting that they were already in possession of that country, and that the war in that section was ended. On receiving this news, General Kearney, who had received by then his promotion, directed Major Sumner, with a portion of the dragoons, to return to the States, and he, with his dragoon escort, pushed forward for California. After a long and tedious journey, he entered the Territory of California in November. Here he learned that a counterrevolution had broken out in California, and sent word to Commodore Stockton to open communications with him. Without waiting for a reply, he pushed forward on December 5, and about forty miles from San Diego met Captain Gillespie, who had come from the shore of the Pacific Ocean to meet him.

It appears that after Stockton and Fremont had taken the Cuidad de los Angeles, and Governor Pico and De Castro had retreated to Sonora, they went north to San Francisco, where they planned an attack upon Acapulco and Mazatlan, on the Pacific side of the Mexican Republic.

Fremont came down the coast with his men, and landing at Monterey, after some difficulty succeeded in providing horses for them, and then marched toward the capital. Matters were in this condition when Kearney reached the Territory.

On his way to join General Kearney, Captain Gillespie learned that a large force of Mexicans was at San Pascual, about fifteen miles from his camp, on another road leading to San Diego. Lieutenant Hammond was sent forward to make a reconnaissance in the evening, and returned about two o'clock on the morning of December 6. He reported that he had found the enemy, but that they had made no effort to pursue him. On learning this, General Kearney decided to attack them. Captain Johnston's First Dragoons, with twelve soldiers, led the advance. They were mounted on the best horses. Captain Moore followed with fifty dragoons, who were mostly mounted on mules, their horses having been broken down in the long march from Santa Fe. Captain Gillespie's volunteers came next; then two mountain howitzers, manned by dragoons, and under command of Lieutenant Davidson; the rest of the troops, including the men from the Pacific squadron under Lieutenant Beall and Passed Midshipman Duncan, of the Navy, remained in rear with the baggage, under Major Swords.

At daybreak on December 6, the enemy was discovered, about one hundred and sixty strong, under Andres Pico, brother of the governor. Captain Johnston immediately charged them, and they gave way. General Kearney followed, with Captain Moore and the other dragoons, when, becoming somewhat scattered, the Mexicans turned rapidly and unexpectedly on their pursuers, and a most bloody conflict ensued, the Mexicans inflicting much damage with their long lances, and having an immense advantage over our men in the fact that their horses were fresh, whereas those of our dragoons were nearly broken down by the long march which they had made. For five minutes the conflict was terrible; but on the approach of the forces in rear, the Mexicans gave way, carrying most of their killed and wounded with them. Lieutenant Davidson was unable to bring his howitzers into action, because at the start of the fight their mules had become frightened and unmanageable.

In this action the Americans lost three officers of the first regiment Dragoons, who were killed. Sixteen noncommissioned officers and privates were also killed or mortally wounded. Brigadier General Kearney was twice severely wounded. For his gallantry at this action he was made a brevet major general.

The Mexicans retired. Captain Henry S. Turner, First Dragoons, took command after General Kearney fell wounded.

The Mexicans appeared in front on the day after the battle, and took post at San Bernardino among the hills, where they seemed inclined to make a stand, but our advance drove them from their position, and then halted. The affairs of General Kearney's command were now in a most critical state. A number of them were wounded, they were all poorly provided for, and surrounded by enemies who were determined to cut them to pieces.

At the rancho of San Bernardino Captain Turner collected some cattle, and sent an express to Commodore Stockton at San Diego asking for assistance. On the night of December 8, Kit Carson, Lieutenant Beall, of the navy, and an Indian servant, volunteered to go to San Diego for assistance from Commodore Stockton. The expedition was one of extreme peril, as the enemy had possession of all of the roads, but, after a night of great hazard and a day of concealment, they reached San Diego, twenty-nine miles distant, in safety.

On the morning of the tenth, Pico attacked Kearney's camp, driving in front of him a drove of horses to protect his men. A few of the horses were killed, and the Mexicans were driven back. Kearney then decided to push on to the ocean on the following day at all hazards, but during the night Lieutenant Grey, of the navy, arrived with reinforcements, and the Americans were relieved. It was just in time as our people were nearly in extremis. They had no provisions, their baggage was gone, for they had burned a portion of it in anticipation of a forward movement, they were without animals, for most of them had been turned loose for want of forage, and with a large number wounded, and considering the strength of the party. It is difficult to conceive how they could have escaped, had it not been for the opportune arrival of Lieutenant Grey. Pico retreated on the junction of Grey's party with Kearney's, and after a weary march, they arrived at San Diego on December 12.

After resting for a time at San Diego, Stockton and Kearney prepared an expedition against the capital, and Stockton, who had been acting as governor, offered to turn over the whole charge of affairs to General Kearney, but this he refused at that time to accept.

Everything being prepared, Stockton and Kearney set out to capture the Cuidad de los Angeles, Kearney acting as commander of the troops, and Stockton accompanying the expedition in the character of governor.

On their approach to the San Gabriel River the enemy was discovered on the opposite bank. This was on January 8, 1847. Here the dragoons, who were serving on foot, behaved well, and the enemy was routed. The next day the force, which consisted of dragoons, sailors, marines, and volunteers, again met the enemy on the Plains of Mesa, near the capital, where another skirmish took place. In this the enemy was again beaten, and on the 10th the American force entered the city. In the meantime, Fremont, who was in the northern portion of California, had organized a body of volunteers, and after a secret march of one hundred and fifty miles, surprised the Mission of San Luis Obispo, capturing the commandant and thirty-five others. The commandant, Don Jesus Pico, was a prisoner on parole at the time of his capture. He was tried by a court-martial and sentenced to death, but this was remitted by Fremont.

After this Lieutenant Colonel Fremont marched to the Cuidad de los Angeles, where he met Stockton and Kearney. The Mexicans by this time saw the futility of their efforts, and, at the convention on the Plains of Couenga, the leaders of the revolt capitulated, and quiet was restored to California. When the troubles with the Mexicans ceased, our own officers commenced quarreling, and a most serious misunderstanding took place as to who was the actual governor. Charges were preferred against Fremont for not obeying Kearney, and both of those officers returned to the States, leaving Colonel Richard B. Mason, First Dragoons, acting as governor, to which place he had been appointed by the President.

Fremont was tried and found guilty of the charges preferred against him, and was sentenced to be dismissed; but the President, in consideration of his valuable services to the country, remitted the sentence. Lieutenant Colonel Fremont was stung by what he considered the injustice done him, and resigned on March 15, 1848.

Mexican Success at Encarnacion

While these events were transpiring on the shores of the Pacific, Brigadier General John E. Wool was organizing a force at San Antonio, Texas, for the purpose of marching upon and capturing the city of Chihuahua, which is the most considerable city in Northwestern Mexico. This force started from San Antonio on September 26.

Upon consultation, Wool turned to the left and marched to Monclova, whence he sent word to General Taylor at Monterey, stating his reasons for not moving forward. Taylor agreed with his views, and, sending a letter to the Secretary of War, asked to have the force under General Wool added to his own, and the expedition to Chihuahua abandoned for the present. The Secretary of War assented to this because the benefits which it was supposed would be derived from the expedition were found to be not at all commensurate with the cost to the government, and Wool's column was added to Taylor's.

Major General Scott visited the Rio Grande in the month of January 1847, and preparatory to his march into the interior, found it necessary to withdraw some of his best troops from General Taylor, leaving enough, however, to protect the valley of the Rio Grande. It was hard for Taylor to part with these men, but the exigencies of the service demanded it, and they started for Tampico and other places en route for Vera Cruz. The greater portion of the dragoons were sent with Scott. After their departure, Taylor, although suffering from mortification at what he supposed was an injustice to him, put his army in the best condition he was able, and advanced to Saltillo. A large Mexican force was believed to be marching upon that place, but as yet no positive evidence of it had been obtained. Before the arrival of the general at Saltillo, a small party of the Arkansas cavalry had been sent out to make such discoveries as were possible, under command of Major Borland. He proceeded some distance, and was about to return, when he was joined by another party of the First Kentucky Cavalry, under Major Gaines and Captain Cassius M. Clay. The parties moved forward to a place called Encarnacion. This was on the night of January 21. General Minon, of the Mexican army, with a large force, was nearby, and learning the exact position of the Americans, quietly surrounded the hacienda where they were encamped, and the next morning all of them were taken prisoners. Two majors, two captains, one lieutenant, and sixty-six cavalry men were captured, and sent as prisoners to the city of Mexico. On the morning of January 26, another party of the Kentucky cavalry, consisting of seventeen men, under Captain Heady, was captured by Lieutenant Colonel Cruz, and was likewise sent to the city of Mexico.

The only man who made his escape at the time Borland's party was taken was Captain Dan Drake Henrie, of Texas, acting as interpreter, who had previously been a prisoner in the hands of the Mexicans, and who believed he would be murdered as soon as he became known to them. When the Americans found they were surrounded, Henrie made known his fears to Major Gaines, and asked him to let him mount his mare, which was known to be very fleet, and a most excellent animal. As the Mexican lancers crowded around, Henrie pretended to be trying to hold the mare, but was, in reality, pressing her against them. They gave way a little for her, which he, discovering, sprang upon her back and darted off. Several shots were fired after him, but the horse was true as steel, and away she went to the mountains. They both escaped, but having no water, this beautiful animal fell dead, and Henrie was obliged to make the best of his way alone. He dared not visit any of the farmhouses along the route, and, after much suffering, reached our army three days after his escape, having had nothing to eat except a mouse or two which he had caught while far off the main road. When found by our people he was almost deranged, and it was a long time before he recovered from the effects of his trials.

General Taylor arrived at Saltillo, and, after staying a short time, moved his force past the rancho of Buena Vista and the pass of L'Angostura to Agua Nueva, where he had a better drillground for his volunteers than he could find elsewhere. In going forward, he had made up his mind, in case of an action coming on, to fall back to the pass of L'Angostura, which was narrow and easily defended, and there give battle to the enemy. Up to this time it was uncertain what the Mexicans intended to do, and no knowledge of the force in front was in Taylor's possession. To make everything secure, and learn as much as possible of the enemy, he sent Brevet Lieutenant Colonel May, with one squadron of the First, one squadron of the Second Dragoons, and some volunteer cavalry, to the rancho of La Hedionda and beyond, to try and discover the enemy. He reached that place on the afternoon of February 20, and thence sent out several parties to scour the country in all directions. In the distance signal fires were seen rising up from the tops of the hills, and to the east clouds of dust indicated the movement of a large body of troops. Second Lieutenant Samuel D. Sturgis, of the dragoons, was sent to the top of a hill to obtain a better view, accompanied by only one dragoon, when both were captured by the enemy and carried off.

May remained out all night, and next morning returned to General Taylor, and announced that the enemy was advancing in force. The next morning, he returned to the field, but in the meantime, the battle had commenced under orders of Generals Wool and Lane. The attack was made by a heavy column of Mexican lancers and infantry, who pushed a portion of our volunteer infantry back, and then attacked the cavalry regiments of Kentucky and Arkansas in the most determined manner; but they withstood the shock, and night put an end to the first day's conflict. On the 23rd another and the final battle was fought, and Santa Anna was forced back, never to appear again on the northern frontier in any considerable numbers. The fight on this day between our cavalry and the Mexican lancers was most deadly, and several of our cavalry officers fell.

This battle, particularly in the West, has been always looked upon as the most severe one ever fought on American soil, and no doubt it was true until the breaking out of the Civil War; still, officers differed in opinion, and many considered Molino del Rey a much more severely contested action. The cavalry made one most gallant charge against the enemy on February 23, and cut their way through them. But the Mexican lancers were far from being a contemptible enemy, and many of them were admirable horsemen. Our people had the advantage of larger horses and heavier men as a general thing, but the Mexicans were much more agile, and could handle their horses as well perhaps as any people on earth. With the lance, they were greatly our superiors, and used that weapon with great effect both at Buena Vista and at San Pascual.

Torrejon and Minon were both good cavalry officers in the Mexican army, and could handle their troops easily. Their forces greatly exceeded ours in numbers, and their irregular troops were no doubt better, as the Mexicans, accustomed as many of them are to a life on horseback, and all of them feeling a pride in owning horse flesh, it did not take so long a time to train them as it did ours, who, particularly those from the older states, know little or nothing about riding or managing horses. The Mexicans are most relentless riders, and their poor horses sometimes suffer dreadfully at their hands.

Scott Invades

Major General Scott landed with his army of invasion near Vera Cruz, Mexico, in March 1847, and, after a somewhat protracted investment and bombardment, that city fell into the hands of the Americans. While the bombardment was going on the dragoons arrived, and refitted above the city, and on the shores of the Gulf of Mexico. The horses were many of them lost in crossing the Gulf, and for many days a portion of the dragoons were dismounted. A fight took place, however, between them and a party of the enemy at the Medelin River, on March 25, 1847. The enemy had been prowling about for several days, when Colonel Harney determined to beat the bush for them. Accordingly, he started, with Thornton's squadron of dragoons and fifty dismounted men, under Captain Ker, in the direction of the river and continued without opposition until near the stone bridge of Morena, which he found fortified, and protected by a force of lancers, with two pieces of artillery. Seeing this, Harney fell back, because he did not have force enough to fight the enemy successfully. As soon as this was known in camp, Captain Hardee, who was disembarking his horses, started with what men he could gather to go to Harney's assistance. Both Thornton and Hardee had been prisoners among the Mexicans, and had been exchanged. Harney, having increased his force by the addition of some volunteers and two pieces of artillery, started on his return to the attack. He formed his infantry on the right and left near the bridge, and Lieutenant Judd, with the cannon, opened fire on the barricades.

This was returned for some time, when he ordered the infantry and dismounted dragoons to charge, and those who were on horseback to follow. The barricade was quickly leaped, but the Mexicans fell back and formed beyond the bridge. Harney ordered it cleared, and sent Sumner with the dragoons across it at a gallop. On their approach the footmen fled into the woods, and the lancers were met and completely routed. Lieutenants Lowry and Oakes pursued a party of lancers some distance, and killed and wounded several of them. Major Sumner and Lieutenant Sibley, with another party of dragoons, pursued another body of lancers, killing and wounding several, as far as the village of Madeline, six miles distant.

Lieutenant Neill, in advance, came up with two lancers, who turned upon him, and inflicted two severe lance wounds upon him, from the effects of which he fell from his horse.

After this the regiments were put in the best shape possible, and the army started on its way to the interior. The progress was slow, as our people were obliged to wait for supplies of every kind to be received from the States, and it was nearly a month before they made much progress. In April, it was known that Santa Anna had taken command of the Mexicans in front of General Scott's army, and had been engaged in throwing up various defenses at Cerro Gordo, on the road to the city of Mexico.

In the battle of Cerro Gordo, on April 17–18, 1847, the dragoons did not play a conspicuous part, as they were not called upon to do anything until the enemy was retreating, when a squadron under Captain Blake, and some companies under Major Beall, pursued the enemy far out on the Jalapa road, and took some prisoners; but the Mounted Rifle regiment behaved most admirably, and won a proud name for itself on that occasion.

On April 17, the first squadron of the regiment, after moving up, was halted about four hundred yards from the point of attack, partly under cover from the enemy's batteries. While waiting, it was fired upon by the batteries and the skirmishers of the enemy. The squadron was deployed, and a charge ordered; at the same time, the rest of the regiment and a company of infantry attacked the enemy on the summit and farther slope of the hill, and they were driven from their position. In this attack, Major Sumner was wounded, and was carried to the rear. The Rifles were then deployed, and, with the First Artillery, drove the enemy from their position. The regiment was then employed in sustaining a battery of mountain howitzers, and in preventing the enemy turning our left. It remained here during the night of the seventeenth, and assisted in placing the heavy guns which were brought up in position. At dawn, it was ordered to prepare for battle. "At an early hour," says Loring, in his report, and before the attack upon the main work, a large succoring force was seen advancing on the Jalapa road. The Rifles were ordered to pass to the left, attract the attention of the enemy, and keep them in check until the storming of the heights commenced, in which the regiment was to join on the left flank. During this diversion, it was exposed to a galling and destructive fire of round, grape, canister, and musketry, upon its front and both flanks, from the enemy's three main entrenchments and batteries, from which it suffered great loss. In this movement, a large force of the enemy was held in check, which from its position, would have been able to have turned the assaulting column. When the general assault was ordered, a portion of the regiment joined in and the works were carried along the whole line, which had been necessarily extended to the left. This accomplished, the regiment, with others, was placed in position on the heights and in a very short time the enemy surrendered. The regiment of Mounted Riflemen followed the retreating army to within ten miles of Jalapa. The total loss to the regiment was seventy-eight killed and wounded.

Mexican Irregulars

The Mexican guerrillas were bodies of men formed, it is believed, by their own government, or sometimes self-constituted, who thought their mission was to annoy and harass our troops as much as possible. They were led by men of the most unscrupulous character, and all laws of war were set aside and disregarded by them. They were most relentless foes, and their operations were carried on with the greatest cruelty toward those who were unfortunate enough to fall into their power. Our men preferred death to getting into their hands, and in our fights with them no quarter was expected on either side.

The costume of these guerrillas was picturesque, and they were generally mounted on horses which, though small, possessed much spirit, and were capable of enduring great fatigue. These horses were descended, no doubt, from those that were brought to that country by the Spaniards during and soon after the conquest of Mexico, and many of them bore traces of Arabian blood. Their progenitors had some of them escaped, or had been reared on the immense plains of Northwestern Mexico or Texas.

The men wore large broad-brimmed hats, which are most unpleasant things to wear in a wind, but which are excellent to shield against the sun's rays. Their jackets were made of leather, velvet, or cloth, and generally embroidered. Their trousers were wide-open at the sides, which were buttoned up by long rows of silver or even gold buttons, and sometimes little bells. They had also tiny bells on their hats and on their immense spurs. Their weapons were a sword, carried under the left leg, whereby it was prevented from dangling, a pistol or two, a short musket, not generally very available; and their lasso, which they threw with amazing dexterity and effect.

They prowled about the American army, annoyed our trains, murdered our soldiers when straggling, and cut to pieces such small parties as they were able to overpower.

Cavalry Operations Near Mexico City

General Scott marched on with his army, and entered the broad and beautiful valley of Mexico in August.

To give a clear and concise view of the part taken by the dragoons at the battles of Contreras and Churubusco on August 20, 1847, I copy Colonel Harney's report, he being commander of the cavalry brigade. Colonel Harney says, in writing at Tacubaya, Mexico, August 24, 1847:

"The cavalry force being necessarily weakened by detachments to the different divisions of the army, I found myself, on the morning of the nineteenth instant, in the immediate command of nine companies only, consisting of six companies of the Second Dragoons, one company of Mounted Riflemen, and two companies of Mounted Volunteers.

"With this force I was ordered by the general-in-chief to report to Brigadier General Twiggs, who was at this time covering Major General Pillow's division in an effort to make a road through the ridge of lava which forms the pass of San Antonio. Owing to the nature of the ground, I was compelled to halt within range of the enemy's shells, and to remain in this position for several hours, an idle spectator of the action which ensued. After night, I returned with my command to San Augustine, and remained there until the enemy's position at Contreras was carried on the morning of the twentieth.

"The reports of Major Sumner, commanding 1st battalion, and Lieutenant Colonel Moore, commanding Second battalion, which I have the honor to forward herewith, will show in what manner the other troops and squadrons of my command were employed. The three troops of horse brought by me on the field being ordered away in different directions, Major Sumner and myself soon found ourselves without commands.

"I then employed myself with my staff in rallying fugitives and encouraging our troops on the left of the main road. Major Sumner, toward the close of the engagement, was placed by the general-in-chief in charge of the last reserve, consisting of the rifle regiment and one company of horse, and was ordered to support the left. This force was moving rapidly to take its position in line of battle, when the enemy

broke and fled to the city. At this moment, perceiving that the enemy were retreating in disorder on one of the main causeways leading to the city of Mexico, I collected all the cavalry within my reach, consisting of parts of Captain Ker's company of Second Dragoons, Captain Kearney's company of First Dragoons, and Captains McReynolds and Duperu's companies of the Third Dragoons, and pursued them vigorously until we were halted by the discharge of the batteries at their gate. Many of the enemy were overtaken in the pursuit, and cut down by our sabers. I cannot speak in terms too complimentary of the manner in which this charge was executed. My only difficulty was in restraining the impetuosity of my men and officers, who seemed to vie with each other who should be foremost in the pursuit. Captain Philip Kearney gallantly led his squadron into the very entrenchments of the enemy, and had the misfortune to lose an arm from a grapeshot fired from a gun at one of the main gates of the capital. Captain McReynolds and Lieutenant Graham were also wounded, and Lieutenant Ewell had two horses shot under him. His death is much to be regretted. On the twentieth, although I had but four companies of my brigade with me on the field, the remainder were actively employed in the performance of important and indispensable duties. Captain Hardee, while watching the enemy with his company near San Augustine, was attacked by a band of guerrillas, but the enemy was promptly and handsomely repulsed, and a number of their horses, with arms and accoutrements, captured."

After the battles of Contreras and Churubusco, an armistice was agreed upon by the authorities, and our army drew its supplies for a time from the city of Mexico itself, pack-mules going in at night and returning laden with rations, etc. This was, of course, done by consent of the Mexican general, and was an understanding at the time the armistice was entered upon. This armistice continued until September 7, when General Scott, believing the Mexicans were acting in bad faith, ordered it to be brought to an end.

Hostilities of an active character commenced soon afterward, and on September 8, 1847, the battle of Molino del Rey was fought. As to the part enacted by the mounted men in that battle, I subjoin Major Sumner's report.

"*My orders were to take a position on the left of our line, to hold in check the enemy's cavalry, and to give a blow to their horse or foot if an opportunity should offer. In taking up my position I was compelled to pass within pistol-shot of a large body of the enemy, who were protected by a ditch and breastworks. This was entirely unavoidable in consequence of a deep ditch on my left, which was impossible to cross until I got very close to their line; and I could not pause at that moment, as a very large body of the enemy's cavalry was advancing toward the left of our line. After passing through this fire and crossing a ravine, I formed my command in line facing the enemy's cavalry, on which they halted, and shortly afterward retired. I continued to hold my command on the left flank of our line until the enemy's infantry broke and retired, changing my position from time to time in order to face their cavalry whenever they advanced. I should have joined in the pursuit of their infantry when they broke; but in doing this I should have uncovered our left, and their large cavalry force was still maintaining a menacing attitude, covered and protected as it was by a large hacienda filled with troops. My loss in passing their line of fire was severe, viz., five officers and thirty-three soldiers wounded, and six soldiers killed; twenty-seven horses killed, and seventy-seven wounded.*

"*Lieutenant Colonel Moore, of the Third Dragoons, joined me after the action commenced, and did me the great favor to abstain from assuming the command. His presence, however, was of great service to me, and his example of the most perfect coolness under fire had a favorable influence upon my command.*

"*Colonel Harney, who was quite unwell, also came upon the field during the action, and, after observing my measures for some time, ex-*

pressed himself satisfied with them, and said to me that he would not assume the command, for which I am deeply obliged to him."

Fall of the City of Mexico

The storming of Chapultepec, which was a strong castle near the city of Mexico, and used as a military school, occurred on September 13, 1847. In this action, as well as along the causeways leading toward the city, and entering it by the Belen Gate, the Mounted Rifle regiment displayed the greatest gallantry. The city was entered and captured on the fourteenth of the same month.

The dragoons had no opportunity of doing much service on entering the city. The loss to the Rifles was, in killed and wounded, seventy-nine.

Major General Scott and his staff, in full uniform, entered the capital at eight o'clock, escorted by Major Sumner with his battalion of cavalry.

When all of the troops had made their way into the city they were sent to their several stations, and the cavalry brigade, under Colonel Harney, was ordered to occupy the cavalry barracks near the National Palace. The city of Mexico was in the possession of the Americans. It is the most ancient as well as the most splendid capital on the American continent, and contained at that time about two hundred thousand inhabitants, and teemed with the white domes of churches and shady *paseos*.

Doniphan's March to Chihuahua

While these events had been transpiring in the valley of Mexico and along the Rio Grande, Colonel Doniphan, with his regiment of Missouri cavalry, had been invading Mexico, and had made a famous march.

When General Kearney left Santa Fe, Doniphan was left at that place with orders to make a campaign against the Navajo Indians, and afterward to join General Wool's column at Chihuahua; it was of course then unknown to both these officers that the proposed expedition to that place under General Wool from San Antonio, Texas, had been broken up, and his forces transferred to General Taylor.

On October 26, 1846, he started from Santa Fe for the invasion of the country occupied by the Navajo Indians. This is a tribe inhabiting the country west of a range of mountains bounding the Rio Grande, and extending down the tributaries of the Rio Colorado to near the Pacific Ocean. The country was invaded by three routes. Every portion of their country was visited; and after near three fourths of them were collected together, a treaty was made with them. It was late in the season; the cold weather came on, and Doniphan's men were obliged to march over a ground covered with snow, and suffering much from intense cold. Finally, however, he reached Valverde, a town on the Rio Grande, in New Mexico, where he refitted, and prepared to set out on his march to Chihuahua.

On December 18, 1846, he left Valverde with his command, which did not exceed eight hundred and fifty-six men, including two small parties which had preceded him. At Donna Ana, his whole force, including Clarke's battery of artillery, was consolidated. On the twenty-fifth, when near Brazito, as he was about to encamp for the night, and the men were bringing in wood and water, the enemy was reported advancing. Soon a messenger, bearing a black flag, from the Mexicans, came into his camp, and demanded his surrender. This was declined, when a smart skirmish took place, and the enemy was beaten back and retired. The loss to both sides was trifling. On the evening of December 27, he entered the town of El Paso, where he remained until the following February, awaiting the arrival of his artillery, with his baggage and provision train. It is hardly fair to call this a battle, but Doniphan and his men considered it so, though his own loss was "none killed, seven wounded, all since recovered." Still, it was a gallant affair, and the Missourians were entitled to much credit.

On the evening of February 8, he left El Paso with a large train for Chihuahua, his own force numbering but little more than one thousand men. His march was undisturbed for several days, but on the twenty-eighth when near the pass of Sacramento, he learned that the enemy in considerable force was waiting for him. This pass is formed by the spur of the mountains which juts down into the plain on the right, and the dry bed of a creek, deep and full of ravines, on the left.

The enemy had considerable artillery well posted, and redoubts had been thrown up under direction of General Garcia Conde, ex-minister of war of Mexico, who was a scientific man, and who had some military knowledge. The artillery was mostly behind these redoubts. The action was commenced by the firing of cannon into the Mexicans, who were drawn up in front of their works. This fire was returned, and the Mexicans retired behind their redoubts. A charge was now ordered by Colonel Doniphan, in which the mounted companies of Captains Reid, Parsons, and Hudson participated, accompanied by two twelve-pounder howitzers under Captain Weightman. The remainder, who had dismounted, followed on foot, and the enemy was soon put to flight. The Mexicans gave way at once, not being able to stand the sabers of our men and the scattering fire of the howitzers. The loss to the Americans was small considering the number engaged, while that of the Mexicans was very considerable.

All of their artillery, consisting of two nine, two eight, four six, and two four pounders, and six culverins, or rampart pieces, was captured, but it does not appear that any of this was very serviceable.

The victory being complete, the Americans entered the city of Chihuahua on March 1, 1847. Here Doniphan remained for some time regulating the affairs of the Mexicans, and resting from his long and tedious march. He moved from this place to Monterey, Mexico, thence to the mouth of the Rio Grande, and thence by water home to St. Louis, Missouri.

Taos

After Doniphan started from Santa Fe, Colonel Sterling Price, of the second regiment of Missouri Cavalry, was left in command. A revolution broke out among the Mexicans, and Governor Charles Bent, and most of the civil officers of the Territory were murdered by them. These murders occurred at the town of Taos, and Price, upon hearing of them, determined not only to punish the rebels, but to capture and put to death the murderers.

Starting from Santa Fe on January 23, 1847, with a battalion of Missouri cavalry, some Santa Fe infantry and two howitzers under Lieutenant Dyer, he continued his course toward Taos until the afternoon of the twenty-fourth, when near the town of Canada, he discovered the enemy in front. Preparations were immediately made for action. Seeing the enemy had possession of a range of hills beyond a creek nearby, he ordered his howitzers to open upon them, and followed with his men at a charge. The enemy gave way, and retreated toward Taos, after having made an unsuccessful attempt to capture the baggage train. The loss to the Americans was not material, and that of the enemy did not appear to frighten them.

On the thirtieth and thirty-first the column continued its march, and on February 1 reached the summit of the Taos Mountain, which was covered with two feet of snow. On the second they encamped near a small village called Rio Chiquito, at the entrance of the valley.

The march had been severe, most of the men had been frostbitten, and all were jaded by the exertions necessary to travel over unbroken roads, which they had necessarily to do to make a path for the baggage wagons and artillery. The men bore everything without a murmur, and on the 3rd marched through Don Fernando de Taos to the Pueblo de Taos, which was found to be a place of great strength, surrounded by adobe walls and strong pickets. Within the enclosure were two large buildings, eight stories high, each capable of sheltering five or six hundred men. Besides these there were several smaller buildings and a large church. The walls were pierced for rifles, and the town was well adapted for defense, every point being flanked by projecting buildings.

On February 4, 1847, after a careful reconnaissance, the attack began with a cannonade of the town from the artillery which kept up a brisk and effective fire. At a given signal, Captain Burgwin, at the head of his own company and that of Captain McMillan, Second Missouri Cavalry, charged the western flank of the church where the enemy had taken a stand, while another party charged the northern wall. As soon as the troops had reached the western flank, axes were used in the attempt to break it; and a temporary ladder having been made, the thatched roof was fired. About this time, Captain Burgwin, at the head of a small party, left the cover afforded by the flank of the church, and, penetrating into the corral in front of that building, endeavored to force the door. In this exposed situation, he was severely wounded. The attempt proved a failure, and they were forced to retire. In the meantime, holes had been cut in the walls of the church, and shells had been thrown in by hand, doing good execution. All this time the enemy had kept up a brisk fire. At about 3:30 p.m., a six-pounder was run up within sixty yards of the church, and after ten rounds, one of the holes which had been cut by the axes was widened into a practicable breach. The gun was now run up within ten yards of the wall, a shell was thrown in, followed by three rounds of grape, when the storming party entered without opposition. The interior of the church was full of smoke, which shielded our men from view of the enemy. They ran out of the church, and many of them fled to the mountains; others took refuge in one of the large houses, and next morning surrendered. The murderers of Governor Bent were captured and punished, as were the leaders of the insurrection.

Rumors of insurrections were rife, and it was said that a large force of Mexicans was marching on Santa Fe from Chihuahua. "I am unable to ascertain," said Price, in his letter to the adjutant general, "whether these rumors are true or false, but it is certain that the New Mexicans entertain deadly hatred against the Americans, and they will cut off small parties of the latter whenever they think they can escape detection."

Now returning to General Scott's line of operations. He was in the city of Mexico; Colonel Childs, with a small garrison, was in the city of Puebla, and all communication with the seaboard was cut off. In this condition of things, it was necessary that something should be done.

Major Folliot T. Lally, of the ninth regiment of Infantry, left Vera Cruz on August 6, 1847, with a mixed command of recruits and parts of regiments, on his way to join General Scott, but his march was harassed at all points by the guerrillas, and he lost many men; finally, after much struggle, he reached the city of Jalapa, where he was forced to halt until reinforcements could be sent to him. This force was a little over one thousand strong, and contained two companies of horse, viz., Captain Loyall's company of Georgia cavalry, and Captain Besangon's company of Louisiana cavalry. During the march, they were not of much service, though several of the men were picked off by the enemy.

Brigadier General Joseph Lane, with his brigade, left Vera Cruz on September 19, 1847, for the city of Mexico. The weather was intensely hot, and his men made slow progress. A party of guerrillas attacked the column on the twentieth, and a company of Louisiana Cavalry, under Captain Lewis, which was his only mounted force, easily routed them, killing and wounding several. On the twenty-second, as the command was starting in the morning, another attack was made by the guerrillas, and a fine young officer named John Kline, who was second lieutenant in Lewis's company, was killed. The guerrillas were again driven off, and did not molest the column any more.

Lane's men were without tents, and in the rains which fell during the latter part of September and in October, they suffered very much.

Fight at Huamantla

At Perote his force was again increased by Captain Samuel H. Walker's company C, regiment of Mounted Riflemen, which was splendidly armed and equipped, and a battalion of infantry. He learned on the 8th of October, while at the hacienda of San Antonio Tamaris, that Santa

Anna, with a large Mexican force, was some twelve miles distant. This Mexican general, after his defeat at the capital, had escaped with a large number of soldiers, and had fallen upon Colonel Childs's garrison at Puebla, which he had been besieging since about September 10. Hearing of Lane's approach, he moved down the Mexican road and fortified the pass of El Final, determined to arrest his farther progress. The ground was admirably chosen, being a high bluff or side of a hill on the left, and a steep declivity on the right of the road; but General Lane did not allow himself to be caught in this very nice trap which had been laid for him. Learning that Santa Anna was off the road at Huamantla, where he could more easily subsist his troops, Lane determined to give him battle there, and thus prevent the Mexican soldiers from guarding the Final Pass.

I was a subaltern in Lane's command at the time, and well recollect the enthusiasm which prevailed among the soldiers at the idea of meeting Santa Anna. Captain Walker, who had had considerable experience, was ordered to take command of the four companies of cavalry, which was really a very respectable body of men. He had orders to lead off, and when he came in sight of the Mexican forces, to wait until the infantry support could come up. The heat was overpowering, but still everybody kept up and when within three miles of the city, Walker discovered a body of Mexicans which he supposed was about equal to his own, and ordering his men to follow, away he went at a gallop. The Mexicans fled toward the town, with Walker and his men streaming after them. The charge of our cavalry was most splendid. The Mexicans could not withstand it, though they fought with their lances with considerable effect. But the Rifles were determined to beat them, and they scattered in all directions. Walker's company did the whole thing, and suffered in consequence most severely. At this time Walker supposed that all was over, and the Mexicans conquered, but in this he was mistaken. A large force of lancers came rolling into town before the American infantry column could get there, and, falling upon Walker's company, some of whom had dismounted to save some pieces of artillery, it was, in effect, cut to pieces. Walker himself was shot down, and died in a few minutes, and his whole cavalry force took refuge in a churchyard. This column of lancers numbered between two and three thousand, and had it not been for the opportune arrival of the infantry, it is a question whether any of the cavalry would have escaped. The fight was now soon over, and the Mexicans, with Santa Anna, started off on their way to Queretaro. This was the last time Santa Anna ever met the Americans in battle, and Lane's infantry had the honor of finishing the military career of this celebrated officer.

The Mexican lancers I saw that day made a most splendid appearance, with their flashing lances, bright pennons, and green uniforms. They were in sight of our column for a considerable time as we were approaching the town at right angles to each other, and each was striving to get there first.

Lane's Night March After Santa Anna

Lane's command returned to Puebla, and a few days afterward he went to the city of Mexico. On the 18th of January, he again started from the capital with one company of Mounted Riflemen, two of the Third Dragoons, and four of Texas Rangers; his object was to capture General Santa Anna, who was known to be in the city of Tehuacan, many miles away. He traveled by night in order to deceive the enemy. On the second night out from Puebla, he encountered a coach with an armed escort. This he halted, but the owner producing a safeguard from the Governor of Mexico, he was obliged to release him. No sooner had Lane left than this Mexican put one of his servants on a mule, and sent him with all haste to Santa Anna, who being apprised of Lane's approach, started from Tehuacan at once.

Lane's party entered the city, but the bird had flown; and after a fruitless search of some hours, he was found to have been too quick for the Americans. This was a sore disappointment, but the soldiers made the best of it by capturing all of Santa Anna's military property, which they carried away as legitimate spoil. Lane captured the town of Tehuacan, the city of Orizaba, and the town of Cordova, killing several enemies, and doing much service. Upon his return, the dragoons, under Major Polk, had a skirmish with a body of guerrillas under Don Manuel Falcon, who were signally defeated.

Learning that a body of guerrillas was infesting the country north and northeast of the capital, he determined, upon his return, to go out and attempt their capture, or, at least, to break up their rendezvous. Accordingly, he started on February 17, 1848, with a command of Mounted Rifles, Third Dragoons, and Texas Rangers, Major Polk again commanding the regular cavalry. Lane found a large body of guerrillas, under Padre Jarauta, at the town of Sequalteplan, and after a spirited skirmish, succeeded in defeating them. Padre Martinez, the second in command, was killed, together with many others. In all of these affairs the mounted men behaved well, and gained considerable reputation. This was the last fight of any importance which occurred in the vicinity of the city of Mexico.

In New Mexico trouble was again brewing, as the country was left nearly barren of mounted men by the expiration of the term of service of the twelve months volunteers. Colonel Price had returned to Missouri with his regiment, but, being appointed brigadier general of volunteers, again went to New Mexico in the autumn of 1847. In the neighboring state of Chihuahua, a Mexican force had been gathered, for the purpose, it was supposed, of attacking the towns of El Paso and Santa Fe. In anticipation of this, Price determined to attack the city of Chihuahua. The enemy was met at Santa Cruz de Rosales, sixty miles from Chihuahua, and the town was stormed on March 16, 1848. Price's command consisted of portions of the first regiment United States Dragoons, and of detachments of Missouri cavalry. The American loss was not great. This was the last act in the war with Mexico, and our soldiers were allowed a period of rest. When the Mexican War closed, the third regiment of Dragoons, which had been raised to serve during the war, was disbanded.

Civil War Cavalry

The battle at Booneville is well worth the study of every cavalry officer, as it was the first fight where Sheridan commanded independent cavalry and is so full of good cavalry tactics that it is here quoted in full.

Sheridan at this time showed a fine conception of the correct use of cavalry. The details of the battle were well known to General Grant and probably had a material influence on Grant when he recommended Sheridan for the command of the cavalry of the Army of the Potomac.

It also resulted in Sheridan's immediate promotion, gave him the command of an infantry division, and brought his qualities to the attention of higher commanders. And who could say that it did not, in this indirect manner, have an important bearing on the destiny of the nation?

As described in Philip Sheridan's Memoirs

Battle at Booneville

On the morning of July 1, 1862, a cavalry command of between five and six thousand men, under the Confederate General James R. Chalmers, advanced on two roads converging near Booneville. The head of the enemy's column on the Blackland and Booneville road came in contact with my pickets three miles and a half west of Booneville. These pickets, under Lieutenant Leonidas S. Scranton, of the Second Michigan Cavalry, fell back slowly, taking advantage of every tree or other cover to fire from till they arrived at the point where the converging roads joined. At this junction, there was a strong position in the protecting timber, and here Scranton made a firm stand, being reinforced presently by a few men he had out as pickets on the road to his left, a second company I had sent him from camp, and subsequently by three companies more, all now commanded by Captain Campbell. This force was dismounted and formed in line, and soon developed that the enemy was present in large numbers. Up to this time Chalmers had shown only the heads of his columns, and we had doubts as to his purpose, but now that our resistance forced him to deploy two regiments on the right and left of the road, it became apparent that he meant business, and that there was no time to lose in preparing to repel his attack.

Full information of the situation was immediately sent me, and I directed Campbell to hold fast, if possible, till I could support him, but if compelled to retire he was authorized to do so slowly, taking advantage of every means that fell in his way to prolong the fighting. Before this I had stationed one battalion of the Second Iowa in Booneville, but Colonel Edward Hatch, commanding that regiment, was now directed to leave one company for the protection of our camp a little to the north of the station, and take the balance of the Second Iowa, with the battalion in Booneville except two saber companies, and form the whole in rear of Captain Campbell, to protect his flanks and support him by a charge should the enemy break his dismounted line.

While these preparations were being made, the Confederates attempted to drive Campbell from his position by a direct attack through an open field. In this they failed, however, for our men, reserving their fire until the enemy came within about thirty yards, then opened on him with such a shower of bullets from our Colt's rifles that it soon became too hot for him and he was repulsed with considerable loss. Foiled in this move, Chalmers hesitated to attack again in front, but began overlapping both flanks of Campbell's line by force of numbers, compelling Campbell to retire toward a strong position I had selected in his rear for a line on which to make our main resistance.

As soon as the enemy saw this withdrawing he again charged in front, but was again as gallantly repelled as in the first assault, although the encounter was for a short time so desperate as to have the character of a hand to hand conflict, several groups of friend and foe using on each other the butts of their guns. At this juncture, the timely arrival of Colonel Hatch with the Second Iowa gave a breathing spell to Campbell, and made the Confederates so chary of direct attacks that he was enabled to retire; and at the same time, I found opportunity to make disposition of the reinforcement to the best advantage possible, placing the Second Iowa on the left of the new line and strengthening Campbell on its right with all the men available.

In view of his numbers, the enemy soon regained confidence in his ability to overcome us, and in a little while again began his flanking movements, his right passing around my left flank some distance, and approaching our camp and transportation, which I had forbidden to be moved out to the rear. Fearing that the enemy would envelop and capture the camp and transportation, I determined to take the offensive. Remembering a circuitous wood road that I had become familiar with, I concluded that the most effective plan would be to pass a small column around the enemy's left, by way of this road, and strike his rear by a mounted charge simultaneously with an advance of our main line on his front. I knew that the attack in rear would be a most hazardous undertaking, but in face of such odds as the enemy had the condition of affairs was most critical, and could be relieved only by a bold and radical change in our tactics; so I at once selected four saber companies, two from the Second Michigan and two from the Second Iowa, and placing Captain Alger, of the former regiment, in command of them,

I informed him that I expected of them the quick and desperate work that is usually imposed on a forlorn hope.

To carry out the purpose now in view, I instructed Captain Alger to follow the wood road as it led around the left of the enemy's advancing forces, to a point where it joined the Blackland road, about three miles from Booneville, and directed him, upon reaching the Blackland road, to turn up it immediately, and charge the rear of the enemy's line. Under no circumstances was he to deploy the battalion, but charge in column right through whatever he came upon, and report to me in front of Booneville, if at all possible for him to get there. If he failed to break through the enemy's line, he was to go ahead as far as he could, and then if any of his men were left, and he was able to retreat, he was to do so by the same route he had taken on his way out. To conduct him on this perilous service I sent along a thin, sallow, tawny-haired Mississippian named Beene, whom I had employed as a guide and scout a few days before, on account of his intimate knowledge of the roads, from the public thoroughfares down to the insignificant bypaths of the neighboring swamps. With such guidance, I felt sure that the column would get to the desired point without delay, for there was no danger of its being lost or misled by taking any of the many byroads which traversed the dense forests through which it would be obliged to pass. I also informed Alger that I should take the reserve and join the main line in front of Booneville for the purpose of making an advance of my whole force, and that as a signal he must have his men cheer loudly when he struck the enemy's rear, in order that my attack might be simultaneous with his.

I gave him one hour to go around and come back through the enemy, and when he started I moved to the front with the balance of the reserve, to put everything I had into the fight. This meant an inestimable advantage to the enemy in case of our defeat, but our own safety demanded the hazard. All along the attenuated line the fighting was now sharp, and the enemy's firing indicated such numerical strength that fear of disaster to Alger increased my anxiety terribly as the time set for the cheering arrived and no sound of it was heard. Relying, however, on the fact that Beene's knowledge of the roads would prevent his being led astray, and confident of Alger's determination to accomplish the purpose for which he set out, as soon as the hour was up I ordered my whole line forward. Fortunately, just at this moment a locomotive and two cars loaded with grain for my horses ran into Booneville from Corinth. I say fortunately, because it was well known throughout the command that in the morning, when I first discovered the large numbers of the enemy, I had called for assistance; and my troops, now thinking that reinforcements had arrived by rail from Rienzi, where a division of infantry was encamped, and inspired by this belief, advanced with renewed confidence and wild cheering. Meantime I had the engineer of the locomotive blow his whistle loudly, so that the enemy might also learn that a train had come; and from the fact that in a few moments he began to give way before our small force, I thought that this stratagem had some effect. Soon his men broke, and ran in the utmost disorder over the country in every direction. I found later, however, that his precipitous retreat was due to the pressure on his left from the Second Iowa, in concert with the front attack of the Second Michigan, and the demoralization wrought in his rear by Alger, who had almost entirely accomplished the purpose of his expedition, though he had failed to come through, or so near that I could hear the signal agreed upon before leaving Booneville.

After Alger had reached and turned up the Blackland road, the first thing he came across was the Confederate headquarters; the officers and orderlies about which he captured and sent back some distance to a farm house. Continuing at a gallop, he soon struck the rear of the enemy's line, but was unable to get through, nor did he get near enough for me to hear his cheering; but as he had made the distance he was to travel in the time allotted, his attack and mine were almost coincident, and the enemy, stampeded by the charges in front and rear, fled toward Blackland, with little or no attempt to capture Alger's command which might readily have been done. Alger's troops soon rejoined me at Booneville, minus many hats, having returned by their original route. They had sustained little loss except a few men wounded and a few temporarily missing. Among these was Alger himself, who was dragged from his saddle by the limb of a tree that, in the excitement of the charge, he was unable to flank. The missing had been dismounted in one way or another, and run over by the enemy in his flight; but they all turned up later, none the worse except for a few scratches and bruises. My effective strength in this fight was 827 all told, and Alger's command comprised ninety officers and men. Chalmers's was composed of six regiments and two battalions, and though I have been unable to find any returns from which to verify his actual numbers, yet, from the statements of prisoners and from information obtained from citizens along his line of march, it is safe to say that he had in action not less than five thousand men. Our casualties were not many—forty-one in all. His loss in killed and wounded was considerable, his most severely wounded—forty men—falling into our hands, having been left at farm houses in the vicinity of the battle field.

The victory in face of such odds was most gratifying; as it justified my disinclination—in fact, refusal—to retire from Booneville without fighting (for the purpose of saving my transportation, as directed by superior authority when I applied in the morning for reinforcements), it was to me particularly grateful. It was also very valuable in view of the fact that it increased the confidence between the officers and men of my brigade and me, and gave us the balance of the month not only comparative rest, but entire immunity from the dangers of a renewed effort to gobble my isolated outpost. In addition to all this, recommendation from my immediate superiors was promptly tendered through oral and written congratulations; and their satisfaction at the result of the battle took definite form a few days later, in an application for my promotion.

Here General Sheridan displayed the same characteristics which he afterwards displayed in the valley. He loved a fight and disobeyed orders to withdraw in order to save his transportation. Here he used a variation of classic cavalry tactics, i.e., holding the enemy in front while a turning movement attacked him simultaneously in rear. He had made a thorough reconnaissance of the surrounding country. He personally knew every road and trail in the vicinity of his camp and utilized them to the best advantage. His outposts were well out and resisted stubbornly until the main body could form for defense. Here we also see a commander playing with the courage of his men, and keeping up their spirits by making them believe in conditions that did not in fact exist.

Custer at Gettysburg
By James Harvey Kidd

By noon, or soon after, the entire division united in the village of Hanover. The First, Fifth, Sixth and Seventh Michigan regiments and Pennington's battery were all on the ground near the railroad station. The Confederate line of battle could be distinctly seen on the hills to the south of the town. The command to dismount to fight on foot was given. The number one, two and three men dismounted and formed in line to the right facing the enemy. The number four men remained with the horses which were taken away a short distance to the rear.

It was here that the brigade first saw Custer. As the men of the Sixth, armed with their Spencer rifles, were deploying forward across the railroad into a wheat field beyond, I heard a voice new to me, directly in rear of the portion of the line where I was, giving directions for the movement, in clear, resonant tones, and in a calm, confident manner, at once resolute and reassuring. Looking back to see whence it came, my eyes were instantly riveted upon a figure only a few feet distant, whose appearance amazed if it did not for the moment amuse me. It was he who was giving the orders. At first, I thought he might be a staff officer, conveying the commands of his chief. But it was at once apparent that he was giving orders, not delivering them, and that he was in command of the line.

Looking at him closely, this is what I saw: an officer superbly mounted who sat his charger as if to the manor born. Tall, lithe, active, muscular, straight as an Indian and as quick in his movements, he had the fair complexion of a school girl. He was clad in a suit of black velvet, elaborately trimmed with gold lace, which ran down the outer seams of his trousers, and almost covered the sleeves of his cavalry jacket. The wide collar of a blue navy shirt was turned down over the collar of his velvet jacket, and a necktie of brilliant crimson was tied in a graceful knot at the throat, the long ends falling carelessly in front. The double rows of buttons on his breast were arranged in groups of twos, indicating the rank of brigadier general. A soft, black hat with wide brim adorned with a gilt cord, and rosette encircling a silver star, was worn turned down on one side giving him a rakish air. His golden hair fell in graceful luxuriance nearly or quite to his shoulders, and his upper lip was garnished with a blonde mustache. A sword and belt, gilt spurs and top boots completed his unique outfit.

A keen eye would have been slow to detect in that rider with the flowing locks and gaudy tie, in his dress of velvet and of gold, the master spirit that he proved to be. That garb, fantastic as at first sight it appeared to be, was to be the distinguishing mark which, during all the remaining years of that war was to show us where, in the thickest of the fight, we were to seek our leader—for where danger was, where swords were to cross, where Greek met Greek, there was he, always. Brave but not reckless; self-confident, yet modest; ambitious, but regulating his conduct at all times by a high sense of honor and duty; eager for laurels, but scorning to wear them unworthily; ready and willing to act, but regardful of human life; quick in emergencies, cool and self-possessed, his courage was of the highest moral type, his perceptions were intuitions. Showy like Murat, fiery like Farnsworth, yet calm and self-reliant like Sheridan, he was the most brilliant and successful cavalry officer of his time. Such a man had appeared upon the scene, and soon we learned to utter with pride the name of—Custer.

George A. Custer was, as all agree, the most picturesque figure of the civil war. Yet his ability and services were never rightly judged by the American people. It is doubtful if more than one of his superior officers—if we except McClellan, who knew him only as a staff subaltern—estimated him at his true value. Sheridan knew Custer for what he was. So did the Michigan brigade and the Third cavalry division. But except by these, he was regarded as a brave, dashing, but reckless officer who needed a guiding hand. Among regular army officers as a class he cannot be said to have been a favorite. The meteoric rapidity of his rise to the zenith of his fame and success, when so many of the youngsters of his years were moving in the comparative obscurity of their own orbits, irritated them. Stars of the first magnitude did not appear often in the galaxy of military heroes. Custer was one of the few.

The popular idea of Custer is a misconception. He was not a reckless commander. He was not regardless of human life. No man could have been more careful of the comfort and lives of his men. His heart was tender as that of a woman. He was kind to his subordinates, tolerant of their weaknesses, always ready to help and encourage them. He was brave as a lion, fought as few men fought, but it was from no love of it. Fighting was his business; and he knew that by that means alone could peace be conquered. He was brave, alert, untiring, a hero in battle, relentless in the pursuit of a beaten enemy, stubborn and full of resources on the retreat. His tragic death at the Little Big Horn crowned his career with a tragic interest that will not wane while history or tradition endure. Hundreds of brave men shed tears when they heard of it—men who had served under and learned to love him in the trying times of civil war.

Custer never would have rushed deliberately on destruction. If, for any reason, he had desired to end his own life, and that is inconceivable, he would not have involved his friends and those whose lives had been entrusted to his care in the final and terrible catastrophe. He was not a reckless commander or one who would plunge into battle with his eyes shut. He was cautious and wary, accustomed to reconnoiter carefully and measure the strength of an enemy as accurately as possible before attacking.

More than once the Michigan brigade was saved from disaster by Custer's caution. Under his skillful hand the four regiments were soon welded into a coherent unit, acting so like one man that the history of one is oftentimes apt to be the history of the other, and it is difficult to draw the line where the credit that is due to one leaves off and that which should be given to another begins.

The result of the day at Hanover was that Stuart was driven still farther away from a junction with Lee. He was obliged to turn to the east, making a wide detour by the way of Jefferson and Dover; Kilpatrick meanwhile maintaining his threatening attitude on the inside of the circle which the redoubtable confederate was traversing, and forcing the latter to swing clear around to the north as far as Carlisle, where he received the first reliable information as to the whereabouts of Lee. It was the evening of July 2 when he finally reached the main army. The battle then had been going on for two days, and the issue was still in doubt. During that day (July 2) both Stuart and Kilpatrick were hastening to rejoin their respective armies, it having been decided that the great battle would be fought out around Gettysburg. Gregg's division had been guarding the right flank of Meade's army, but at nightfall it was withdrawn to a position on the Baltimore pike near the reserve artillery.

Kilpatrick reached the inside of the union lines, in the vicinity of Gettysburg, late in the afternoon, at about the same hour that Hampton, with Stuart's leading brigade, arrived at Hunterstown, a few miles northeast of Gettysburg. It was about five o'clock in the afternoon when the Third division, moving in column of fours, was halted temporarily, awaiting orders where to go in, and listening to the artillery firing close in front, when a staff officer rode rapidly along the column, crying out: "Little Mac is in command and we are whipping them." It was a futile attempt to evoke enthusiasm and conjure victory with the magic of McClellan's name. There was scarcely a faint attempt to cheer. There was no longer any potency in a name.

Soon thereafter, receiving orders to move out on the road to Abbottstown, Kilpatrick started in that direction, Custer's brigade leading, with the Sixth Michigan in advance. When nearing the village of Hunterstown, on a road flanked by fences, the advance encountered a heavy force of confederate cavalry. A mounted line was formed across the road, while there were dismounted skirmishers behind the fences on either side. The leading squadron of the Sixth, led by Captain H. E. Thompson, boldly charged down the road, and at the same time, three troops were dismounted and deployed on the ridge to the right, Pennington's battery going into position in their rear. The mounted charge was a most gallant one, but Thompson, encountering an overwhelmingly superior force in front, and exposed to a galling fire on both flanks, as he charged past the confederates behind the fences, was driven back, but not before he himself had been severely wounded, while his first lieutenant, S. H. Ballard, had his horse shot under him and was left behind a prisoner. As Thompson's squadron was retiring, the enemy attempted a charge in pursuit, but the dismounted men on the right of the road kept up such a fusillade with their Spencer carbines, aided by the rapid discharges from Pennington's battery, that he was driven back in great confusion.

The position at Hunterstown was held until near midnight when Kilpatrick received orders to move to Two Taverns, on the Baltimore turnpike, about five miles southeast of Gettysburg, and some three miles due south from the Rummel farm, on the Hanover road, east of Gettysburg, where the great cavalry fight between Gregg and Stuart was to take place on the next day. It was three o'clock in the morning

(Kilpatrick says "daylight") when Custer's brigade went into bivouac at Two Taverns.

The Second cavalry division, commanded by General D. McM. Gregg, as has been seen, held the position on the Rummel farm on the second but was withdrawn in the evening to the Baltimore pike "to be available for whatever duty they might be called upon to perform on the morrow." On the morning of the third, Gregg was ordered to resume his position of the day before, but states in his report that the First and Third brigades (McIntosh and Irvin Gregg) were posted on the right of the infantry, about three-fourths of a mile nearer the Baltimore and Gettysburg pike, because he learned that the Second brigade (Custer's) of the Third division was occupying his position of the day before. General Kilpatrick, in his report says:

> *"At 11:00 p.m. (July 2) received orders to move (from Hunterstown) to Two Taverns, which point we reached at daylight. At 8:00 a.m. (July 3) received orders from headquarters cavalry corps to move to the left of our line and attack the enemy's right and rear with my whole command and the reserve brigade. By some mistake, General Custer's brigade was ordered to report to General Gregg and he (Custer) did not rejoin me during the day."*

General Custer, in his report, gives the following, which is without doubt, the true explanation of the "mistake." He says:

> *"At an early hour on the morning of the third, I received an order through a staff officer of the brigadier general commanding the division (Kilpatrick), to move at once my command and follow the First brigade (Farnsworth) on the road leading from Two Taverns to Gettysburg. Agreeably to the above instructions, my column was formed and moved out on the road designated, when a staff officer of Brigadier General Gregg, commanding the Second division, ordered me to take my com-*

mand and place it in position on the pike leading from York (Hanover)
to Gettysburg, which position formed the extreme right of our line of
battle on that day."

Thus, it is made plain that there was no "mistake" about it. It was
Gregg's prescience. He saw the risk of attempting to guard the right
flank with only the two decimated brigades of his own division. Seeing
with him was to act. He took the responsibility to intercept Kilpatrick's
rear and largest brigade, turn it off the Baltimore pike, to the right, instead of allowing it to go to the left, as it had been ordered to do, and
thus, doubtless, a serious disaster was averted. It makes one tremble to
think what might have been, of what inevitably must have happened,
had Gregg, with only the two little brigades of McIntosh and Irvin
Gregg and Randol's battery, tried to cope single-handed with the four
brigades and three batteries, comprising the very flower of the confederate cavalry and artillery, which Stuart, Hampton and Fitzhugh Lee
were marshaling in person on Cress's ridge.

If Custer's presence on the field was, as often has been said, "prov-
idential," it is General D. McM. Gregg to whom, under Providence,
the credit for bringing him there was due. If, at Gettysburg, the Michigan cavalry brigade won honors that will not perish, it was to Gregg
that it owed the opportunity, and his guiding hand it was that made
its blows effective. It will be seen how, later in the day, he again boldly
took responsibility at a critical moment and held Custer to his work
on the right, even after the latter had been ordered by higher authority
than himself (Gregg) to rejoin Kilpatrick and after Custer had begun
the movement. Now, having admitted, that Gregg did the planning, it
will be shown how gallantly Custer and his Michigan brigade did their
part of the fighting. Up to a certain point, it will be best to let General
Custer tell his own story:

"Upon arriving at the point designated, I immediately placed my com-

mand in a position facing toward Gettysburg. At the same time, I caused reconnaissances to be made on my front, right and rear, but failed to discover any considerable force of the enemy. Everything remained quiet until 10:00 a.m., when the enemy appeared on my right flank and opened upon me with a battery of six guns. Leaving two guns and a regiment to hold my first position and cover the road leading to Gettysburg, I shifted the remaining portion of my command forming a new line of battle at right angles with my former position. The enemy had obtained correct range of my new position, and was pouring solid shot and shell into my command with great accuracy. Placing two sections of battery "M," Second regular artillery, in position, I ordered them to silence the enemy's battery, which order, notwithstanding the superiority of the enemy's position, was done in a very short space of time. My line as it then existed, was shaped like the letter "L." The shorter branch, supported by one section of battery "M" (Clark's), supported by four squadrons of the Sixth Michigan cavalry, faced toward Gettysburg, covering the pike; the long branch, composed of the two remaining sections of battery "M," supported by a portion of the Sixth Michigan cavalry on the left, and the First Michigan cavalry on the right—with the Seventh Michigan cavalry still further to the right and in advance—was held in readiness to repel any attack on the Oxford (Low Dutch) road. The Fifth Michigan was dismounted and ordered to take position in front of my center and left. The First Michigan was held in column of squadrons to observe the movements of the enemy. I ordered fifty men to be sent one mile and a half on the Oxford (Low Dutch) road, and a detachment of equal size on the York (Hanover) road, both detachments being under the command of the gallant Major Weber (of the Sixth) who, from time to time, kept me so well informed of the movements of the enemy, that I was enabled to make my dispositions with complete success."

General Custer says further, that at twelve o'clock he received an order directing him, on being relieved by a brigade of the Second division, to move to the left and form a junction with Kilpatrick; that on the arrival of Colonel McIntosh's brigade he prepared to execute the order; but, to quote his own language:

> *"Before I had left my position, Brigadier General Gregg, commanding the Second division, arrived with his entire command. Learning the true condition of affairs, and rightly conjecturing the enemy was making his dispositions for vigorously attacking our position, Brigadier General Gregg ordered me to remain in the position I then occupied."*

So much space has been given to these quotations because they cover a disputed point. It has been claimed, and General Gregg seems to countenance that view, that Custer was withdrawn and that McIntosh, who was put in his place, opened the fight, after which Gregg brought Custer back to reinforce McIntosh. So far from this being true, it is quite the reverse of the truth. Custer did not leave his position. The battle opened before the proposed change had taken place, and McIntosh was hurried in on the right of Custer. The latter was reluctant to leave his post—knew he ought not to leave it. He had already been attacked by a fire from the artillery in position beyond the Rummel buildings. Major Weber, who was out on the crossroad leading northwest from the Low Dutch road, had observed the movement of Stuart's column, headed by Chambliss and Jenkins, past the Stallsmith farm, to the wooded crest behind Rummel's, and had reported it to Custer. Custer did, indeed, begin the movement. A portion of the Sixth Michigan and, possibly, of the Seventh, also, had begun to withdraw when Custer met Gregg coming on the field and explained to him the situation—that the enemy was "all around" and preparing to "push things." Gregg told him to remain where he was and that portion of the brigade which was moving away halted, countermarched, and reoccupied its former position. The Fifth Michigan had not been withdrawn from the line in front, and Pennington's guns had never ceased to thunder their responses to the confederate challenge.

Custer says that the enemy opened upon him with a battery of six guns at 10:00 a.m. Stuart, on the contrary, claims to have left Gettysburg about noon. It is difficult to reconcile these two statements. A good deal of latitude may be given the word "about," but it is probable that the one puts the hour too early, while the other does not give it early enough; for, of course, before Custer could be attacked, some portion of Stuart's command must have been upon the field.

Official reports are often meager, if not sometimes misleading, and must needs be reinforced by the memoranda and recollections of actual participants, before the exact truth can be known.

Major Charles E. Storrs, of the Sixth Michigan, who commanded a squadron, was sent out to the left and front of Custer's position, soon after the brigade arrived upon the ground. He remained there several hours and was recalled about noon—he is positive it was later than twelve—to take position with the troops on the left of the battery. He states that the first shot was not fired until sometime after his recall, and he is sure it was not earlier than two o'clock.

When Stuart left Gettysburg, as he says about noon, he took with him Chambliss's and Jenkins's brigades of cavalry and Griffin's battery. Hampton and Fitshugh Lee were to follow; also, Breathed's and McGregor's batteries, as soon as the latter had replenished their ammunition chests. Stuart moved two and a half miles out on the York turnpike, when he turned to the right by a country road that runs southeasterly past the Stallsmith farm. (This road intersects the Low Dutch road, about three-fourths of a mile from where the latter crosses the Hanover pike.) Turning off from this road to the right, Stuart posted the brigades of Jenkins and Chambliss and Griffin's battery on the commanding Cress's ridge, beyond Rummel's and more than a mile from the position occupied by Custer. This movement was noticed by Major Weber, who with his detachment of the Sixth Michigan cavalry, was stationed in the woods northeast of Rummel's, where he could look out on the open country beyond, and he promptly reported the fact to Custer.

The first shot that was fired came from near the wood beyond Rummel's. According to Major McClellan, who was assistant adjutant general on Stuart's staff, this was from a section of Griffin's Battery, and was aimed by Stuart himself, he not knowing whether there was anything in his front or not. Several shots were fired in this way.

Major McClellan is doubtless right in this, that these shots were fired as feelers; but it is inconceivable that Stuart was totally unaware of the presence of any federal force in his immediate front; that he did not know that there was stationed on the opposite ridge a brigade of cavalry and a battery. Gregg had been there the day before, and Stuart at least must have suspected, if he did not know, that he would find him there again. It is probable that he fired the shots in the hope of drawing out and developing the force he knew was there, to ascertain how formidable it might be, and how great the obstacle in the way of his farther progress toward the rear of the union lines.

The information he sought was quickly furnished. It was then that Custer put Pennington's battery in position, and the three sections of rifled cannon opened with a fire so fast and accurate that Griffin was speedily silenced and compelled to leave the field.

Then there was a lull. I cannot say how long it lasted but, during its continuance, General Gregg arrived and took command in person. About this time, also, it is safe to say that Hampton and Fitzhugh Lee came up and took position on the left of Chambliss and Jenkins. The confederate line then extended clear across the federal front, and was screened by the two patches of woods between Rummel's and the Stallsmith farm.

A battalion of the Sixth Michigan cavalry, of which mine was the leading troop, was placed in support and on the left of Pennington's battery. This formed, at first, the short line of the "L" referred to in Custer's report, but it was subsequently removed farther to the right and faced in the same general direction as the rest of the line, where it remained until the battle ended. Its duty there was to repel any attempt that might be made to capture the battery.

The ground upon which these squadrons were stationed overlooked the plain, and the slightest demonstration in the open ground from either side was immediately discernible. From this vantage ground it was possible to see every phase of the magnificent contest that followed. It was like a spectacle arranged for us to see. We were in the position of spectators at joust or tournament where the knights, advancing from their respective sides, charge full tilt upon each other in the middle of the field.

The lull referred to was like the calm that precedes the storm. The troopers were dismounted, standing "in place rest" in front of their horses, when suddenly there burst upon the air the sound of that terrific cannonading that preceded Pickett's charge. The earth quaked. The tremendous volume of sound volleyed and rolled across the intervening hills like reverberating thunder in a storm.

It was then between one and two o'clock. (Major Storrs says after two.) It was not long thereafter, when General Custer directed Colonel Alger to advance and engage the enemy. The Fifth Michigan, its flanks protected by a portion of the Sixth Michigan on the left, by McIntosh's brigade on the right, moved briskly forward towards the wooded screen behind which the enemy was known to be concealed. In this movement, the right of regiment was swung well forward, the left somewhat "refused," so that Colonel Alger's line was very nearly at right angles with the left of Stuart's position.

As the Fifth Michigan advanced from field to field and fence to fence, a line of gray came out from behind the Rummel buildings and the woods beyond. A stubborn and spirited contest ensued. The opposing batteries filled the air with shot and shrieking shell. Amazing marksmanship was shown by Pennington's battery, and such accurate artillery firing was never seen on any other field. Alger's men with their eight shotted carbines, forced their adversaries slowly but surely back, the gray line fighting well and superior in numbers, but unable to withstand the storm of bullets. It made a final stand behind the strong line of fences, in front of Rummel's and a few hundred yards out from the foot of the slope whereon, concealed by the woods, Stuart's reserves were posted.

While the fight was raging on the plain, Weber with his outpost was driven in. His two troops were added to the four already stationed on the left of Pennington's battery. Weber, who had been promoted to major but a few days before, was ordered by Colonel Gray to assume command of the battalion. As he took his place by my side in front of the leading troop, he said: "I have seen thousands of them over there," pointing to the front. "The country yonder, is full of the enemy."

He had observed all of Stuart's movements, and it was he who gave Custer the first important information as to what the enemy was doing; which information was transmitted to Gregg, and probably had a determining influence in keeping Custer on the field.

Weber was a born soldier, fitted by nature and acquirements for much higher rank than any he held. Although but twenty-three years of age, he had seen much service. A private in the Third Michigan infantry in 1861, he was next battalion adjutant of the Second Michigan cavalry, served on the staff of General Elliott, in the southwest, and came home with Alger in 1862, to take a troop in the Sixth Michigan cavalry. The valuable service rendered by him at Gettysburg was fitly recognized by Custer in his official report. He was killed ten days later at Falling Waters, while leading his squadron in a charge which was described by Kilpatrick as "the most gallant ever made." Anticipating a spirited fight, he was eager to have a part in it. "Bob," he said to me a few days before, while marching through Maryland, "I want a chance to make one saber charge." He thought the time had come. His eye flashed and his face flushed as he watched the progress of the fight, fretting and chafing to be held in reserve when the bugle was summoning others to the charge.

The Fifth Michigan, holding the most advanced position, suffered greatly, Hampton having reinforced the confederate line. Among those killed at this stage of the battle was Major Noah H. Ferry, of the Fifth. Repeating rifles are not only effective but wasteful weapons as well, and Colonel Alger, finding that his ammunition had given out, felt compelled to retire his regiment and seek his horses. Seeing this, the enemy sprang forward with a yell. The union line was seen to yield. The puffs of smoke from the muzzles of their guns had almost ceased. It was plain the Michigan men were out of ammunition and unable to maintain the contest longer. On from field to field, the line of gray followed in exultant pursuit. Breathed and McGregor opened with redoubled violence. Shells dropped and exploded among the skirmishers, while thicker and faster they fell around the position of the reserves. Pennington replied with astonishing effect, for every shot hit the mark, and the opposing artillerists were unable to silence a single union gun. But still they came, until it seemed that nothing could stop their victorious career. "Men, be ready," said Weber. "We will have to charge that line." But the course of the pursuit took it toward the right, in the direction of Randol's battery where Chester was serving out canister with the same liberal hand displayed by Pennington's lieutenants, Clark, Woodruff and Hamilton.

Just then, a column of mounted men was seen advancing from the right and rear of the union line. Squadron succeeded squadron until an entire regiment came into view, with sabers gleaming and colors gaily fluttering in the breeze. It was the Seventh Michigan, commanded by Colonel Mann. Gregg, seeing the necessity for prompt action, had given the order for it to charge. As the regiment moved forward, and cleared the battery, Custer drew his saber, placed himself in front and shouted: "Come on you Wolverines!" The Seventh dashed into the open field and rode straight at the dismounted line which, staggered by the appearance of this new foe, broke to the rear and ran for its reserves. Custer led the charge half way across the plain, then turned to the left;

but the gallant regiment swept on under its own leaders, riding down and capturing many prisoners.

There was no check to the charge. The squadrons kept on in good form. Every man yelled at the top of his voice until the regiment had gone, perhaps, five or six hundred yards straight towards the confederate batteries, when the head of column was deflected to the left, making a quarter turn, and the regiment was hurled headlong against a post-and-rail fence that ran obliquely in front of the Rummel buildings. This proved for the time an impassable barrier. The squadrons coming up successively at a charge, rushed pell-mell on each other and were thrown into a state of indescribable confusion, though the rear troops, without order or orders, formed left and right front into line along the fence, and pluckily began firing across it into the faces of the confederates who, when they saw the impetuous onset of the Seventh thus abruptly checked, rallied and began to collect in swarms upon the opposite side. Some of the officers leaped from their saddles and called upon the men to assist in making an opening. Among these were Colonel George G. Briggs, then adjutant, and Captain H. N. Moore. The task was a difficult and hazardous one, the posts and rails being so firmly united that it could be accomplished only by lifting the posts, which were deeply set, and removing several lengths at once. This was finally done, however, though the regiment was exposed not only to a fire from the force in front, but to a flanking fire from a strong skirmish line along a fence to the right and running nearly at right angles with the one through which it was trying to pass.

While this was going on, Briggs's horse was shot and he found himself on foot, with three confederate prisoners on his hands. With these he started to the rear, having no remount. Before he could reach a place of safety, the rush of charging squadrons from either side had intercepted his retreat. In the melee that followed, two of his men ran away, the other undertook the duty of escorting his captor back to the confederate lines. The experiment cost him his life, but the plucky adjutant, although he did not "run away," lived to fight again on many "another day."

In the meantime, through the passageway thus effected, the Seventh moved forward, the center squadron leading, and resumed the charge. The confederates once more fell back before it. The charge was continued across a plowed field to the front and right, up to and past Rummel's, to a point within 200 or 300 yards of the confederate battery. There another fence was encountered, the last one in the way of reaching the battery, the guns of which were pouring canister into the charging column as fast as they could fire. Two men, privates Powers and Inglede, of Captain Moore's troop, leaped this fence and passed several rods beyond. Powers came back without a scratch, but Inglede was severely wounded. These two men were, certainly, within 200 yards of the confederate cannon.

But, seeing that the enemy to the right had thrown down the fences, and was forming a column for a charge, the scattered portions of the Seventh began to fall back through the opening in the fence. Captain Moore, in whose squadron sixteen horses had been killed, retired slowly, endeavoring to cover the retreat of the dismounted men but, taking the wrong direction, came to the fence about 100 yards above the opening, just as the enemy's charging column struck him. Glancing over his shoulder, he caught the gleam of a saber thrust from the arm of a sturdy confederate. He ducked to avoid the blow, but received the point in the back of his head. At the same time, a pistol ball crashed through his charger's brain and the horse went down, Moore's leg under him. An instant later, Moore avenged his steed with the last shot in his revolver, and the confederate fell dead at his side. Some dismounted men of the Thirteenth Virginia cavalry took Moore prisoner and escorted him back to the rear of their battery, from which position, during the excitement that followed, he made his escape.

But now Alger who, when his ammunition gave out, hastened to his horses, had succeeded in mounting one battalion, commanded by

Major L. S. Trowbridge, and when the Ninth and Thirteenth Virginia struck the flank of the Seventh Michigan, he ordered that officer to charge and meet this new danger. Trowbridge and his men dashed forward with a cheer, and the enemy in their turn were put to flight. Past the Rummel buildings, through the fields, almost to the fence where the most advanced of the Seventh Michigan had halted, Trowbridge kept on. But he, too, was obliged to retire before the destructive fire of the confederate cannon, which did not cease to belch forth destruction upon every detachment of the union cavalry that approached near enough to threaten them. The major's horse was killed, but his orderly was close at hand with another and he escaped. When his battalion was retiring it, also, was assailed in flank by a mounted charge of the First Virginia cavalry, which was met and driven back by the other battalion of the Fifth Michigan led by Colonel Alger.

Then, as it seemed, the two belligerent forces paused to get their second breath. Up to that time, the battle had raged with varying fortune. Victory, that appeared about to perch first on one banner, and then on the other, held aloof, as if disdaining to favor either. The odds, indeed, had been rather with the confederates than against them, for Stuart managed to outnumber his adversary at every critical point, though Gregg forced the fighting, putting Stuart on his defense, and checkmating his plan to fight an offensive battle. But the wily confederate had kept his two choicest brigades in reserve for the supreme moment, intending then to throw them into the contest and sweep the field with one grand, resistless charge.

All felt that the time for this effort had come, when a body of mounted men began to emerge from the woods on the left of the confederate line, northeast of the Rummel buildings, and form column to the right as they debouched into the open field. Squadron after squadron, regiment after regiment, orderly as if on parade, came into view, and successively took their places.

Then Pennington opened with all his guns. Six rifled pieces, as fast as they could fire, rained shot and shell into that fated column. The effect was deadly. Great gaps were torn in that mass of mounted men, but the rents were quickly closed. Then, they were ready. Confederate chroniclers tell us there were two brigades—eight regiments—under their own favorite leaders. In the van, floated a stand of colors. It was the battle flag of Wade Hampton, who with Fitzhugh Lee was leading the assaulting column. In superb form, with sabers glistening, they advanced. The men on foot gave way to let them pass. It was an inspiring and an imposing spectacle, that brought a thrill to the hearts of the spectators on the opposite slope. Pennington double-shotted his guns with canister, and the head of the column staggered under each murderous discharge. But still it advanced, led on by an imperturbable spirit, that no storm of war could cow.

Meantime, the Fifth Michigan had drawn aside a little to the left, making ready to spring. McIntosh's squadrons were in the edge of the opposite woods. The Seventh was sullenly retiring with faces to the foe. Weber and his battalion and the other troops of the Sixth were on edge for the fray, should the assault take the direction of Pennington's battery which they were supporting.

On and on, nearer and nearer, came the assaulting column, charging straight for Randol's battery. The storm of canister caused them to waver a little, but that was all. A few moments would bring them among Chester's guns who, like Pennington's lieutenants, was still firing with frightful regularity, as fast as he could load. Then Gregg rode over to the First Michigan, and directed Town to charge. Custer dashed up with similar instructions, and as Town ordered sabers to be drawn, placed himself by his side, in front of the leading squadron.

With ranks well closed, with guidons flying and bugles sounding, the grand old regiment of veterans, led by Town and Custer, moved forward to meet that host, outnumbering it three to one. First at a trot, then the command to charge rang out, and with gleaming saber and flashing pistol. Town and his heroes were hurled right in the teeth of Hampton and Fitzhugh Lee. Alger, who with the Fifth had been waiting for the right moment, charged in on the right flank of the column as it passed, as did some of McIntosh's squadrons, on the left. One troop of the Seventh, led by Lieutenant Dan Littlefield, also joined in the charge.

Then it was steel to steel. For minutes—and for minutes that seemed like years—the gray column stood and staggered before the blow; then yielded and fled. Alger and McIntosh had pierced its flanks, but Town's impetuous charge in front went through it like a wedge, splitting it in twain, and scattering the confederate horsemen in disorderly rout back to the woods from whence they came.

During the last melee, the brazen lips of the cannon were dumb. It was a hand-to-hand encounter between the Michigan men and the flower of the southern cavaliers, led by their favorite commanders.

Stuart retreated to his stronghold, leaving the union forces in possession of the field.

The rally sounded, the lines were reformed, the wounded were cared for, and everything was made ready for a renewal of the conflict. But the charge of the First Michigan ended the cavalry fighting on the right at Gettysburg. Military critics have pronounced it the finest cavalry charge made during that war.

Custer's brigade lost one officer (Major Ferry) and twenty-eight men killed; eleven officers and 112 men wounded; 67 men missing; total loss, 219. Gregg's division lost one man killed; seven officers and nineteen men wounded; eight men missing; total, thirty-five. In other words, while Gregg's division, two brigades, lost thirty-five, Custer's single brigade suffered a loss of 219. These figures apply to the fight on July 3, only. The official figures show that the brigade, during the three days, July 1, 2 and 3, lost one officer and thirty-one men killed; thirteen officers and 134 men wounded; seventy-eight men missing; total, 257.

For more than twenty years after the close of the civil war, the part played by Gregg, Custer and McIntosh and their brave followers in the battle of Gettysburg received but scant recognition. Even the maps prepared by the corps of engineers stopped short of Cress's Ridge and Rummel's fields. History was practically silent on the subject, and had not the survivors of those commands taken up the matter, there might have been no record of the invaluable services which the Second cavalry division and Custer's Michigan brigade rendered at the very moment when a slight thing would have turned the tide of victory the other way. In other words, the decisive charge of Colonel Town and his Michiganders coincided in point of time with the failure of Pickett's assault upon the center, and was a contributing cause in bringing about the latter result.

With Sheridan in the Shenandoah Valley

By Wesley Merritt

Up to the summer of 1864 the Shenandoah Valley had not been to the Union armies a fortunate place either for battle or for strategy. A glance at the map will go far toward explaining this. The Valley has a general direction from southwest to northeast. The Blue Ridge Mountains, forming its eastern barrier, are well defined from the James River above Lynchburg to Harper's Ferry on the Potomac. Many passes (in Virginia called "gaps") made it easy of access from the Confederate base of operations; and bordered by a fruitful country filled with supplies, it offered a tempting highway for an army bent on a flanking march on Washington or the invasion of Maryland or Pennsylvania. For the Union armies, while it was an equally practicable highway, it led away from the objective, Richmond, and was exposed to flank attacks through the gaps from vantage-ground and perfect cover.

It was not long after General Grant completed his first campaign in Virginia, and while he was in front of Petersburg, that his attention was called to this famous seat of side issues between Union and Confederate armies. With quick military instinct, he saw that the Valley was not useful to the Government for aggressive operations. He decided that it must be made untenable for either army. In doing this he reasoned that the advantage would be with us, who did not want it as a source of supplies, nor as a place of arms, and against the Confederates, who wanted it for both. Accordingly, instructions were drawn up for carrying on a plan of devastating the Valley in a way "least injurious to the people." These instructions, which were intended for Hunter, were destined to be carried out by another, and how well this was accomplished it is my purpose to recount.

Hunter's failure to capture Lynchburg in the spring of 1864 and his retreat by a circuitous line opened the Valley to General Early, who had gone to the relief of Lynchburg. Marching down the Valley and taking possession of it without serious opposition, Early turned Harper's Ferry, which was held by a Union force under Sigel, and crossed into Maryland at Shepherdstown. The governors of New York, Pennsylvania, and Massachusetts were called on for hundred-days men to repel the invasion, and later the Army of the Potomac supplied its quota of veterans as a nucleus around which the new levies could rally. General Early marched on Washington, and on July 11 was in front of the gates of the capital. The following day, after a severe engagement in which the guns of Fort Stevens took part, he withdrew his forces through Rockville and Poolesville, and, crossing the Potomac above Leesburg, entered the Valley of Virginia through Snicker's Gap. Afterward, crossing the Shenandoah at the ferry of the same name, he moved to Berryville, and there awaited developments.

After the immediate danger to Washington had passed it became a question with General Grant and the authorities in Washington to select an officer who, commanding in the Valley, would prevent further danger from invasion. After various suggestions, Major-General Philip H. Sheridan was selected temporarily for this command.

Naturally, on assuming command, Sheridan moved with caution. He was incited to this by his instructions, and inclined to it by his unfamiliarity with the country, with the command, and with the enemy he had to deal with. On the other hand, Early, who had nothing of these to learn, save the mettle of his new adversary, was aggressive, and at once maneuvered with a bold front, seemingly anxious for a battle. The movements of the first few days showed, however, that Early was not disposed to give battle unless he could do so on his own conditions.

On the morning of August 10, Sheridan, who had massed his army at Halltown, in front of Harper's Ferry, marched toward the enemy's communications, his object being to occupy Early's line of retreat and force him to fight before reinforcements could reach him. The march of my cavalry toward the Millwood–Winchester road brought us in contact with the enemy's cavalry on that road, and it was driven toward Kernstown. At the same time a brigade under Custer, making a reconnaissance on the Berryville–Winchester road, came on the enemy holding a defile of the highway while his trains and infantry were marching toward Strasburg. As soon as the retreat of the enemy was known to General Sheridan the cavalry was ordered to pursue and harass him. Near White Post, Devin came upon a strongly posted force, which, after a sharp fight, he drove from the field, and the division took position on the Winchester–Front Royal pike. The same day my division had a severe affair with infantry near Newtown, in which the loss to my Second Brigade was considerable.

On August 12, the enemy having retired the night before, the cavalry pursued to Cedar Creek, when it came up with Early's rearguard and continued skirmishing until the arrival of the head of the infantry column. The day following, the reconnaissance of a brigade of cavalry discovered the enemy strongly posted at Fisher's Hill. About this time Early received his expected reinforcements. General Sheridan, being duly informed of this, made preparations to retire to a position better suited for defense and adapted to the changed conditions of the strength of the two armies.

On August 13, General Devin's brigade of the First Division was ordered to Cedarville on the Front Royal pike, and on the fourteenth I marched with the rest of my division to the same point, Gibbs taking position near Nineveh. On the arrival of his reinforcements Early had requested General R. H. Anderson, in command, to take station at Front Royal, it being a convenient point from which to make a flank movement in case of attack on Sheridan's command, which Early undoubtedly contemplated. At the same time, it constituted a guard to the Luray Valley.

About 2:00 p.m. on the 16th an attack was made by this command on the First Cavalry Division, which resulted in the battle of Cedarville. A force of cavalry under Fitz Lee, supported by a brigade of Kershaw's division, made a descent on Devin's brigade. General Fitz Lee drove in the cavalry pickets and attacked Devin with great violence. This force was scarcely repulsed when a brigade of infantry was discovered moving on the opposite bank of the Shenandoah River toward the left of the cavalry position. One regiment of Custer's brigade, dismounted, was moved up to the crest of a hill near the riverbank to meet this force, while the rest of the brigade, mounted, was stationed to the right of the hill. At the same time the Reserve Brigade under General Gibbs was summoned to the field. The enemy advanced boldly, wading the river, and when within short carbine range was met by a murderous volley from the dismounted men, while the remainder of the command charged mounted. The Confederates were thrown into confusion and retreated, leaving three hundred prisoners, together with two stand of colors. Anderson hurried reinforcements to his beaten brigades, but no further attempt to cross the river was made. The loss to the Union cavalry was about sixty in killed and wounded. The loss to the enemy was not less than five hundred.

These affairs between the Union cavalry and the enemy's infantry were of more importance than might appear at first glance. They gave the cavalry increased confidence, and made the enemy correspondingly doubtful even of the ability of its infantry, in anything like equal numbers, to contend against our cavalry in the open fields of the Valley.

On the night of the sixteenth, Sheridan withdrew toward his base, and on the following day the cavalry marched, driving all the cattle and livestock in the Valley before it, and burning the grain from Cedar Creek to Berryville. No other private property was injured, nor were families molested.

On the afternoon of the seventeenth, the Third Division of cavalry, under General James H. Wilson, reported to General Torbert, chief-of-cavalry, who with it and Lowell's brigade and the Jersey brigade (Penrose's) of the Sixth Corps was ordered to cover the flank of the army which marched and took position near Berryville. General Early, who on the morning of the 17th discovered the withdrawal of Sheridan's force, pursued rapidly, Anderson advancing from Front Royal with his command. Early struck Torbert's force with such vigor and with such overwhelming numbers as completely to overthrow it, with considerable loss, and drive it from Winchester. In this affair, Penrose's brigade lost about three hundred men in killed, wounded, and prisoners, and Wilson's cavalry lost in prisoners some fifty men. At this time, information having reached Sheridan that the reinforcements that had come to Early under Anderson were only part of what might be expected, Sheridan concluded still further to solidify his lines. On August 21, Early moved with his army to attack Sheridan. His own command marched through Smithfield toward Charlestown, and Anderson on the direct road through Summit Point. Rodes's and Ramseur's infantry were advanced to the attack, and heavy skirmishing was continued for some time with a loss to the Sixth Corps, principally Getty's division, of 260 killed and wounded. In the meantime, Anderson was so retarded by the Union cavalry that he did not reach the field, and night overtaking him at Summit Point, he there went into camp. That night Sheridan drew in the cavalry, and, carrying out the resolution already formed, withdrew his army to Halltown. During the three days following, the Confederates demonstrated in front of Sheridan's lines, but to little purpose except to skirmish with Crook's and Emory's pickets. On

Lt. Col. William Washington commanded
the 3rd Continental Light Dragoons.

Dragoons attack infantry in the
Revolutionary War.

Lee's Legion skirmishing at
Gilford Court House.

May charging with his dragoons at the Battle of Resaca.

Early daguerreotype of U.S. dragoons in Mexico.

U.S. dragoons under fire in the Mexican War.

U.S. dragoons charge Mexican lancers at the Battle of Buena Vista.

Custer's charge at Gettysburg.

Watering the horses.

Winslow Homer's watercolor sketch of the 6th Pennsylvania,
the only U.S. Cavalry unit to employ lances.

Cavalry charge in columns of four.

Union cavalry charge.

Sitting Bull and Custer.

Troopers fighting dismounted.

Rough Riders.

For the honor of the troop.

the 25th, leaving Anderson's force in front of Sheridan, Early moved with his four divisions and Fitzhugh Lee's cavalry to Leetown, from which place he dispatched Lee toward Williamsport while he crossed the railroad at Kearneysville and moved toward Shepherdstown. Between Kearneysville and Leetown he was met by Torbert with the cavalry. A sharp fight followed, in the first shock of which Early's advance, consisting of Wharton's division, was driven back in confusion, but upon discovering the strength of the enemy, Torbert withdrew in good order, though Custer's brigade was pressed so closely that he was forced to cross the Potomac. A charge on the flank of the pursuing infantry relieved Custer from danger, and the next morning he returned, as ordered, via Harper's Ferry to the army at Halltown. Early's movement ended with this affair, and during the following two days he returned to the vicinity of Winchester.

During the absence of Early, R. H. Anderson's position was reconnoitered by Crook with two divisions and Lowell's cavalry brigade, who carried Anderson's lines, driving two brigades from their earthworks and capturing a number of officers and men, after which Anderson withdrew from Sheridan's front.

In a dispatch to Halleck, Sheridan said: "I have thought it best to be prudent, everything considered." Grant commended Sheridan's conduct of affairs in general terms, and predicted the withdrawal from the Valley of all of Early's reinforcements. This the pressure of Grant's lines at Petersburg finally accomplished.

On August 28, Sheridan moved his army forward to Charlestown. My division of cavalry marched to Leetown, and drove the enemy's cavalry to Smithfield and across the Opequon. The next day Early's infantry, in turn, drove my division from Smithfield; whereupon Sheridan, advancing with Ricketts's division, repulsed the enemy's infantry, which retired to the west bank of the Opequon. On this day, the cavalry had some severe fighting with Early's infantry, but not until in hand-to-hand fighting the Confederate cavalry had been driven from the field.

On September 3, Rodes's Confederate division proceeded to Bunker Hill, and in conjunction with Lomax's cavalry made a demonstration which was intended to cover the withdrawal of Anderson's force from the Valley. But on marching toward the gap of the Blue Ridge, via Berryville, Anderson came upon Crook's infantry just taking station there. The meeting was a surprise to both commands and resulted in a sharp engagement which continued till nightfall. On the following morning Early moved with part of his infantry to Anderson's assistance, and demonstrating toward the right of Sheridan's lines, he made show of giving battle, but only long enough to extricate Anderson and his trains, when the entire command retired to the country near Winchester. On the fourteenth Anderson withdrew from Early's army, and this time unmolested pursued his march through the Blue Ridge to Culpeper Court House. Fitzhugh Lee's cavalry remained with Early.

About this time General Grant visited the Valley and found everything to his satisfaction. Sheridan was master of the situation, and he was not slow in showing it to his chief. On September 12, Sheridan had telegraphed Grant to the effect that it was exceedingly difficult to attack Early in his position behind the Opequon, which constituted a formidable barrier; that the crossings, though numerous, were deep, and the banks abrupt and difficult for an attacking force; and, in general, that he was waiting for the chances to change in his favor, hoping that Early would either detach troops or take some less defensible position. His caution was fortunate at this time, and his fearlessness and hardihood were sufficiently displayed thereafter. In the light of criticisms, then, it is curious that the world is now inclined to call Sheridan reckless and foolhardy.

At 2:00 a.m. on September 19, Sheridan's army was astir under orders to attack Early in front of Winchester. My cavalry was to proceed to the fords of the Opequon, near the railroad crossing, and, if opposed only by cavalry, was to cross at daylight and, turning to the left, attack Early's left flank. Wilson's division was to precede the infantry and clear the crossing of the Opequon, on the Berryville road, leading to Winchester. The infantry of the army, following Wilson, was to cross the Opequon, first Wright and then Emory, while Crook's command, marching across country, was to take position in reserve, or be used as circumstances might require. South of Winchester, running nearly east and emptying into the Opequon, is Abraham's Creek, and nearly parallel to it, on the north of Winchester, is Red Bud Creek. These two tributaries flanked the usual line of the Confederates, when in position, covering Winchester, and on this line, across the Berryville–Winchester road, Ramseur was stationed with his infantry, when Sheridan's forces debouched from the defile and deployed for attack. Sheridan's plan was to attack and overthrow this part of Early's force before the rest of the army, which a day or two before was known to be scattered to the north as far as Martinsburg, could come to its assistance. At daylight, Wilson advanced across the Opequon, and carried the earthwork which covered the defile and captured part of the force that held it. The infantry followed—Wright's corps first, with Getty leading, and Emory next. Between two and three miles from the Opequon, Wright came up with Wilson, who was waiting in the earthwork he had captured. There the country was suitable for the deployment of the column, which commenced forming line at once.

Ramseur, with the bulk of the Confederate artillery, immediately opened on Wright's troops, and soon the Union guns were in position to reply. Wilson took position on the left of the Sixth Corps. Then followed a delay that thwarted the part of the plan which contemplated the destruction of Early's army in detail. Emory's command was crowded off the road in its march, and so delayed by the guns and trains of the Sixth Corps that it was slow getting on the field, and it was hours before the lines were formed. This delay gave the Confederates time to bring up the infantry of Gordon and Rodes. Gordon, who first arrived, was posted on Ramseur's left near the Red Bud, and when Rodes arrived with three of his four brigades, he was given the center. This change in the situation, which necessitated fighting Early's army in his chosen position, did not disconcert the Union commander. He had come out to fight, and though chafing at the unexpected delay, fight he would to the bitter end.

In the meantime, the cavalry, which had been ordered to the right, had not been idle. Moving at the same time as did the rest of the army, my division reached the fords of the Opequon near the railroad crossing at early dawn. Here I found a force of cavalry supported by Breckinridge's infantry. After sharp skirmishing the stream was crossed at three different points, but the enemy contested every foot of the way beyond. The cavalry, however, hearing Sheridan's guns, and knowing the battle was in progress, was satisfied with the work it was doing in holding from Early a considerable force of infantry. The battle here continued for some hours, the cavalry making charges on foot or mounted according to the nature of the country, and steadily though slowly driving the enemy's force toward Winchester. Finally, Breckinridge, leaving one brigade to assist the cavalry in retarding our advance, moved to the help of Early, arriving on the field about two p.m.

It was 11:30 a.m. before Sheridan's lines were ready to advance. When they moved forward, Early, who had gathered all his available strength, met them with a front of fire, and the battle raged with the greatest fury. The advance was pressed in the most resolute manner, and the resistance by the enemy being equally determined and both sides fighting without cover, the casualties were very great. Wright's infantry forced Ramseur and Rodes steadily to the rear, while Emory on the right broke the left of the enemy's line and threw it into confusion. At this time the Confederate artillery opened with canister at short range, doing fearful execution. This, coupled with the weakening of the center at the junction between Emory and Wright, and with a charge delivered on this junction of the lines by a part of Rodes's command, just arrived on the field, drove back the Union center. At this critical moment Russell's division of Wright's corps moved into the breach on Emory's left, and, striking the flank of the Confederate troops who were pursuing Grover, restored the lines and stayed the Confederate advance. The loss to both sides had been heavy. General Russell of the Union army and Generals Rodes and Godwin of the Confederate were among the killed.

A lull in the battle now followed, which General Sheridan improved to restore his lines and to bring up Crook, who had not yet been engaged. It had been the original purpose to use Crook on the left to assist Wilson's cavalry in cutting off Early's retreat toward Newtown. But the stress of battle compelled Sheridan to bring his reserve in on the line, and accordingly Crook was ordered up on Emory's right, one brigade extending to the north of Red Bud Creek. At the same time, Early reformed his lines, placing Breckinridge's command in reserve. At this time Merritt, who with his cavalry had followed Breckinridge closely to the field, approached on the left rear of the Confederates, driving their flying and broken cavalry through the infantry lines. The cavalry then charged repeatedly into Early's infantry, first striking it in the rear, and afterward face to face as it changed front to repel the attack. These attacks were made by the cavalry without any knowledge of the state of the battle except what was apparent to the eye. First Devin charged with his brigade, returning to rally, with three battle flags and over three hundred prisoners. Next Lowell charged with his brigade, capturing flags, prisoners, and two guns. After this the entire division was formed and charged to give the final coup.

At the time of this last charge the Union infantry advanced along the entire line and the enemy fled in disorder from the field, and night alone (for it was now dark) saved Early's army from capture.

At daylight on the morning of the twentieth the army moved rapidly up the main Valley road in pursuit of the enemy. Early had not stopped on the night of the battle until he reached the shelter of Fisher's Hill. This is admirably situated for defense for an army resisting a movement south. Here the Valley is obstructed by the Massanutten

Mountains and its width virtually reduced to four or five miles. In this position, Early's right was protected by impassable mountains and by the north fork of the Shenandoah, and he at once took means to protect his left artificially.

"On the evening of the twentieth," reports Sheridan, "Wright and Emory went into position on the heights of Strasburg, Crook north of Cedar Creek, the cavalry on the right and rear of Emory, extending to the back road."

On the twenty-first, Sheridan occupied the day in examining the enemy's lines and improving his own. Accompanied by General Wright, he directed changes in the lines of the Sixth Corps, so that it occupied the high lands to the north of Tumbling Run. Wright did not secure this vantage-ground without a severe struggle, in which Warner's brigade was engaged, finally holding the heights after a brilliant charge. Sheridan decided on turning Early's impregnable position by a movement on the Little North Mountain. On the night of the twenty-first, he concealed Crook's command in the timber north of Cedar Creek. In making his disposition Sheridan did not attempt to cover the entire front, it being his intention to flank the enemy by Crook's march, and then, by advancing the right of Wright's and Emory's line, to form connection and make his line continuous. On the morning of the twenty-second, Crook, being still concealed, was marched to the timber near Little North Mountain and massed in it. Before this, Torbert, with his two divisions of cavalry, except one brigade (Devin's), was ordered via Front Royal into Luray Valley, with a view to reentering the Valley of the Shenandoah at New Market. This design was not accomplished.

Not long before sundown Crook's infantry, which had not yet been discovered by the enemy, struck Early's left and rear so suddenly as to cause his army to break in confusion and flee. The rout was complete, the whole of Sheridan's troops uniting in the attack. That night, though the darkness made the marching difficult, Sheridan followed

Early as far as Woodstock, some fifteen miles, and the following day up to Mount Jackson, where he drove the enemy, now to some extent reorganized, from a strong position on the opposite bank of the river. From this point the enemy retreated in line of battle. But every effort to make him fight failed. No doubt Sheridan in this pursuit regretted the absence of his cavalry, which, with Torbert, was striving, by a circuitous and obstructed march, to reach the enemy's rear.

A few miles beyond New Market Early abandoned the main road, which leads on through Harrisonburg; turning to the east, he pursued the road that leads thence to Port Republic. This direction was taken to receive the reinforcements which were to reach him through one of the gaps of the Blue Ridge. For it appears that Kershaw and his command had not proceeded beyond Culpeper in his march to Lee's army before he was ordered to return to Early, the news of whose overthrow at Winchester, and afterward at Fisher's Hill, had reached the authorities at Richmond.

On September 25, Torbert with the cavalry rejoined General Sheridan, and was at once put to work doing what damage was possible to the Central Railway. After proceeding to Staunton and destroying immense quantities of army stores, Torbert moved to Waynesboro, destroying the railway track, and after burning the railway bridges toward the Blue Ridge, and on being threatened by Early's forces, which had moved thither to attack him, he retired to Bridgewater.

Naturally a question now arose between Sheridan, the authorities in Washington, and General Grant as to the future theater of the campaign and the line of operations. Sheridan was opposed to the proposition submitted by the others, which was to operate against Central Virginia from his base in the Valley. The general reasons for his opposition were the distance from the base of supplies; the lines of communication, which in a country infested by guerrillas it would take an army to protect; and the nearness, as the campaign progressed, if successful, to the enemy's base, from which large reinforcements could easily and secretly be hurried and the Union army be overwhelmed. But before the plan was finally adopted a new turn was given to affairs, and the plan originally formed was delayed in its execution if not changed altogether.

When the army commenced its return march, the cavalry was deployed across the Valley, burning, destroying, or taking away everything of value, or likely to become of value, to the enemy. It was a severe measure, and appears severer now in the lapse of time; but it was necessary as a measure of war. The country was fruitful and was the paradise of bushwhackers and guerrillas. They had committed numerous murders and wanton acts of cruelty on all parties weaker than themselves. Officers and men had been murdered in cold blood on the roads, while proceeding without a guard through an apparently peaceful country. The thoughtless had been lured to houses only to find, when too late, that a foe was concealed there, ready to take their lives if they did not surrender. It is not wonderful, then, that the cavalry sent to work the destruction contemplated did not at that time shrink from the duty. It is greatly to their credit that no personal violence on any inhabitant was ever reported, even by their enemies. The Valley from Staunton to Winchester was completely devastated, and the armies thereafter occupying that country had to look elsewhere for their supplies. There is little doubt, however, that enough was left in the country for the subsistence of the people, for this, besides being contemplated by orders, resulted of necessity from the fact that, while the work was done hurriedly, the citizens had ample time to secrete supplies, and did so.

The movement north was conducted without interruption for two days, except that the enemy's cavalry, made more bold by the accession to its strength of a command under General T. L. Rosser, followed our cavalry, dispersed across the Valley. On October 8, the enemy's cavalry harassed Custer's division on the back road during the day, taking from him some battery-forges and wagons. The cavalry also showed itself on the main road upon which Merritt was retiring, but dispersed upon being charged by a brigade which was sent to develop their strength. That night Sheridan gave orders to his chief-of-cavalry, Torbert, to attack and beat the enemy's cavalry the following day "or to get whipped himself," as it was expressed.

On the morning of the ninth, Torbert's cavalry moved out to fight that of the enemy under Generals Rosser and Lomax. Merritt's division moved on the pike and extended across to the back road where Custer was concentrated. A stubborn cavalry engagement commenced the day, but it was not long before the Confederate cavalry was broken and routed, and from that time till late in the day it was driven a distance of twenty-six miles, losing everything on wheels, except one gun, and this at one time was in possession of a force too weak to hold it. At one time, General Lomax was a prisoner, but made his escape by personally overthrowing his captor. In this affair, the advantage of pluck, dash, and confidence, as well as of numbers, was on the Union side. From the time of the occupation of the Valley by Sheridan's force the cavalry had been the active part of his command. Scarcely a day passed that they were not engaged in some affair, and often with considerable loss, as is shown by the fact that in twenty-six engagements, aside from the battles, the cavalry lost an aggregate of 3,205 men and officers.

In reporting the result of the cavalry battle of October 9, Early says:

"This is very distressing to me, and God knows I have done all in my power to avert the disasters which have befallen this command; but the fact is the enemy's cavalry is so much superior to ours, both in numbers and equipment, and the country is so favorable to the operations of cavalry, that it is impossible for ours to compete with his."

He further says in this same connection:

"Lomax's cavalry is armed entirely with rifles and has no sabers, and

the consequence is they cannot fight on horseback, and in this open coun-
try they cannot successfully fight on foot against large bodies of cavalry."

This is a statement on which those who think our cavalry never fought mounted and with the saber should ponder. The cavalry had scant justice done it in reports sent from the battlefield; and current history, which is so much made up of first reports and first impressions, has not to a proper extent been impressed with this record.

On the return of the army after the pursuit of the scattered remnants of Early's force, General Sheridan placed it in position on Cedar Creek north of the Shenandoah, Crook on the left, Emory in the center, and Wright in reserve. The cavalry was placed on the flanks. The occupation of Cedar Creek was not intended to be permanent; there were many serious objections to it as a position for defense. The approaches from all points of the enemy's stronghold at Fisher's Hill were through wooded ravines in which the growth and undulations concealed the movement of troops, and for this reason and its proximity to Fisher's Hill the pickets protecting its front could not be thrown, without danger of capture, sufficiently far to the front to give ample warning of the advance of the enemy. We have already seen how Sheridan took advantage of like conditions at Fisher's Hill. Early was now contemplating the surprise of his antagonist.

On October 12, Sheridan received a dispatch from Halleck saying that Grant wished a position taken far enough south to serve as a base for operations upon Gordonsville and Charlottesville. On the thirteenth and the sixteenth, he received dispatches from the Secretary of War and from General Halleck pressing him to visit Washington for consultation.

On the fifteenth, General Sheridan, taking with him Torbert with part of the cavalry, started for Washington, the design being to send the cavalry on a raid to Gordonsville and vicinity. The first camp was made near Front Royal, from which point the cavalry was returned to the army, it being considered safer to do so in consequence of a dispatch intercepted by our signal officers from the enemy's station on Three Top Mountain, and forwarded to General Sheridan by General Wright.

This dispatch was as follows:

"To Lieutenant-General Early: Be ready to move as soon as my forces join you, and we will crush Sheridan.
—Longstreet, Lieutenant-General."

In sending back the cavalry General Sheridan wrote to General Wright, directing caution on his part, so that he might be duly prepared to resist the attack in case the above dispatch was genuine. Sheridan continued to Washington, and the cavalry resumed its station in the line of defense at Cedar Creek. At this time, everything was quiet—suspiciously so.

On the sixteenth, Custer made a reconnaissance in his front on the back road, but found no enemy outside the lines at Fisher's Hill. This absence of the enemy's cavalry was accounted for the next morning just before daylight by the appearance of Rosser in the rear of Custer's picket line with his cavalry and one brigade of infantry. Rosser carrying the infantry behind his cavalry troopers had made a march of thirty-two miles to capture an exposed brigade of Custer's division on the right; but a change in the arrangements of the command (the return of Torbert) thwarted the scheme, and it resulted only in the capture of a picket guard. On the eighteenth, reconnaissance on both flanks discovered no sign of a movement by the enemy.

The result of the destruction of supplies in the Valley was now being felt by Early's troops. About this time he writes: "I was now compelled to move back for want of provisions and forage, or attack the enemy in his position with the hope of driving him from it; and I determined to attack." From reports made by General Gordon and a staff-officer who ascended Three Top Mountain to reconnoiter the Union position, and the result of a reconnaissance made at the same time by General Pegram toward the right flank of the Union army, General Early concluded to attack by secretly moving a force to turn Sheridan's left flank at Cedar Creek.

The plan of this attack was carefully made; the routes the troops were to pursue, even after the battle had commenced, were carefully designated. The attack was made at early dawn. The surprise was complete. Crook's camp, and afterward Emory's, were attacked in flank and rear and the men and officers driven from their beds, many of them not having the time to hurry into their clothes, except as they retreated half awake and terror-stricken from the overpowering numbers of the enemy. Their own artillery, in conjunction with that of the enemy, was turned on them, and long before it was light enough for their eyes, unaccustomed to the dim light, to distinguish friend from foe, they were hurrying to our right and rear intent only on their safety. Wright's infantry, which was farther removed from the point of attack, fared somewhat better, but did not offer more than a spasmodic resistance. The cavalry on the right was on the alert. The rule that in the immediate presence of the enemy the cavalry must be early prepared for attack resulted in the whole First Division being up with breakfast partly finished, at the time the attack commenced. A brigade sent on reconnaissance to the right had opened with its guns some minutes before the main attack on the left, for it had met the cavalry sent by Early to make a demonstration on our right.

The disintegration of Crook's command did not occupy many minutes. With a force of the enemy passing through its camp of sleeping men, and another powerful column well to their rear, it was not wonderful that the men as fast as they were awakened by the noise of battle thought first and only of saving themselves from destruction. The advance of Gordon deflected this fleeing throng from the main road to the rear, and they passed over to the right of the army and fled along the back road. Emory made an attempt to form a line facing along the main road, but the wave of Gordon's advance on his left, and the thunders of the attack along the road from Strasburg, rendered the position untenable, and he was soon obliged to withdraw to save his lines from capture.

At this time, there were hundreds of stragglers moving off by the right to the rear, and all efforts to stop them proved of no avail. A line of cavalry was stretched across the fields on the right, which halted and formed a respectable force of men, so far as numbers were concerned, but these fled and disappeared to the rear as soon as the force which held them was withdrawn. By degrees the strength of the battle died away. The infantry of the Sixth Corps made itself felt on the advance of the enemy, and a sort of confidence among the troops which had not fled from the field was being restored. A brigade of cavalry was ordered to the left to intercept the enemy's advance to Winchester. Taylor's battery of artillery, belonging to the cavalry, moved to the south, and, taking position with the infantry which was retiring, opened on the enemy. The artillery with the cavalry was the only artillery left to the army. The other guns had either been captured or sent to the rear. This battery remained on the infantry lines and did much toward impeding the enemy's advance until the cavalry changed position to the Winchester–Strasburg road. This change took place by direction of General Torbert about ten o'clock. In making it the cavalry marched through the broken masses of infantry direct to a point on the main road northeast of Middletown. The enemy's artillery fire was terrific. Not a man of the cavalry left the ranks unless he was wounded, and everything was done with the precision and quietness of troops on parade. General Merritt informed Colonel Warner of Getty's division, near which the cavalry passed, and which was at that time following the general retreat of the army, of the point where the cavalry would take position and fight, and Warner promised to notify General Getty, and no doubt did so, for that division of the Sixth Corps advanced to the position on the cavalry's right. Then

Devin and Lowell charged and drove back the advancing Confederates. Lowell dismounted his brigade and held some stonewalls whose position was suited to defense. Devin held on to his advance ground. Here the enemy's advance was checked for the first time, and beyond this it did not go.

The enemy's infantry sheltered themselves from our cavalry attacks in the woods to the left, and in the enclosures of the town of Middletown. But they opened a devastating fire of artillery. This was the state of affairs when Sheridan arrived.

Stopping at Winchester overnight on the eighteenth, on his way from Washington, General Sheridan heard the noise of the battle the following morning, and hurried to the field. His coming restored confidence. A cheer from the cavalry, which awakened the echoes of the valley, greeted him and spread the good news of his coming over the field.

He rapidly made the changes necessary in the lines, and then ordered an advance. The cavalry on the left charged down on the enemy in their front, scattering them in all directions. The infantry, not to be outdone by the mounted men, moved forward in quick time and charged impetuously the lines of Gordon, which broke and fled. It took less time to drive the enemy from the field than it had for them to take it. They seemed to feel the changed conditions in the Union ranks, for their divisions broke one after another and disappeared toward their rear. The cavalry rode after them and over them, until night fell and ended the fray at the foot of Fisher's Hill. Three battle flags and twenty-two guns were added to the trophies of the cavalry that day. Early lost almost all his artillery and trains, besides everything that was captured from the Union army in the morning.

The battle of Cedar Creek has been immortalized by poets and historians. The transition from defeat, rout, and confusion to order and victory, and all this depending on one man, made the country wild with enthusiasm.

Third Battle at Winchester

By William H. Beach

September 17, part of the regiment was on picket at Portersfield. The reserve was in some thick woods near a ford of the Opequon. The posts were so placed as to cover a considerable front. For greater security patrols passed frequently from one post to another. Late in the evening, George G. Peavey and Pliny F. Nelson were patrolling. It was a little past full moon, and the moon, an hour or so high, threw the shadows of some woods on the right beyond the middle of the road. All seemed quiet. But the two men were watchful, and the actions of their horses excited their suspicions. They drew and cocked their revolvers, and rode on. Suddenly they found themselves in the midst of a large number of men who stepped out from the shadows of the woods and quickly closed around them. They were surrounded. In suppressed voices the Confederates commanded the two men to surrender. To Peavey the quick thought came, "We can surrender and save our lives, but the reserve will be surprised and captured or slain. By firing, we may lose our lives, but we will give the alarm and save the reserve." Quick as the thought he poured the fire of his revolver among the enemy. Nelson did the same. They wheeled their horses and, lying low, dashed through the line that had formed around them. The enemy fired a volley after them.

Peavey escaped unharmed. Nelson's horse was shot and he himself received two shots in the breast. The next day he was taken to the general hospital at Sandy Hook. The bullets were removed, but he suffered terrible agony, and on the nineteenth he died. He was an honest man and a faithful soldier.

The Confederates did not linger. Traces of blood on the ground indicated that Peavey's and Nelson's shots had done some execution. Their wounded they took with them, except one. He had been shot through the body and left behind. In his pocket was found the following:

Headquarters, Army Northern Virginia,
8 August, 1864.

Private D. I. Lewis, Co. B, 12th Virginia Cavalry, will proceed to Jefferson County, Virginia, to procure a fresh horse, returning in twenty (20) days without fail.

By command of General R. E. Lee,
H. B. McClellan,
A. A. General.

This pass was kept in Peavey's family as a trophy. The wounded man recovered and was held a long time as a prisoner. This fearless firing of Peavey's in the face of almost certain death was one more heroic act added to many previous ones.

This picket force remained on duty the next day, and at midnight was called back to Leetown where the rest of the regiment was resting in the woods near the Episcopal church.

Grant had made a visit to Sheridan. The latter explained to his chief the situation and his plans. Grant was well satisfied, and asked Sheridan when he would be ready to move. The reply was satisfactory, and Grant took his leave, impressed with the other's confidence that he was going to win.

Sheridan had been waiting to hear from a girl in Winchester. The girl transmitted her intelligence by writing on a piece of tissue paper. This she folded in tin foil. This again she covered up in a convenient quantity of tobacco which she gave to a trusty colored man whose innocent appearance enabled him to get through the lines without exciting suspicion. A part of Early's force, Kershaw's, had been detached, and this was the news that Sheridan had been waiting to hear.

At 2:00 a.m. on the morning of the nineteenth, the whole army was astir. Averell's division moved toward Martinsburg and then along the pike toward Winchester. It was familiar ground, ground that had been hotly contested time and again. It was yet early morning when the enemy was found. Again, in parallel columns of squadrons at such distances from each other that, moving "front into line," the columns could quickly be transformed into one continuous line reaching far out across the fields on both sides of the pike, with a skirmish line thrown out in front, the division steadily advanced. The enemy fought stubbornly, but was steadily forced back. All the forenoon and till the middle of the afternoon was this hot fighting kept up. The line was then not far from Stephenson's Depot.

Far off to the left had been heard the continuous roll of infantry and the heavier roar of artillery. All of Sheridan's army was engaged, and as it had crowded forward, the great semicircle along which the fight began, had contracted, and Merritt's right was now in touch with Averell's left.

The force in front of Averell was Fitz Hugh Lee's cavalry supported by Breckinridge's infantry. There was a feeling of satisfaction over the way in which things were evidently going. The division had fought its way to a position on "high vantage ground" from which could be seen, across the plain toward Winchester, the long lines of Lee's horsemen seeming as if, after the long day's hunt, they had been brought to bay.

The First New York was directed to fall back a little and rest in reserve. The men who had been in the saddle constantly since before daybreak, opened ranks, dismounted, and rested themselves by walking about, but not getting far away from their horses which kept their places in the ranks. They were not out of reach of the enemy's fire. Now and then a solid shot would come bounding and rolling along among the men and horses. From an advanced position on their skirmish line, protected in an angle of a stonewall, a few Confederate riflemen were sending their minie balls wherever they could see a fair mark.

A young Irishman, because of his five years' experience in the regular cavalry and his good service as a drill sergeant, had been made a lieutenant. While he had done some good service, there had been times when, in critical situations, he had shown symptoms of nervousness. There were men like the captain who some time before this had resigned, brave enough at times, at other times not so brave. It had been said of this captain when a detachment was just starting on a charge, "He would have got into that fight in spite of himself if he had not succeeded by main strength in holding in his horse."

While the rest of the men had dismounted, this lieutenant had preferred to remain in his saddle. Although not a tall man, he sat high on his horse, and was a good mark for those Confederate riflemen. As some of those minie balls whizzed past uncomfortably close to his head, he involuntarily dodged. Again, the bullets came, and again he ducked his head. The men laughed, and some remarks were made. The minies became malicious, and the men laughed again until the lieutenant turned upon them in his towering wrath, "Who's a hootin'? (duck) Who's a hootin'? (duck) Who's this a hootin'? (duck) Some of yeez'll be a hootin' (duck) to yer sorra yit!" His manner of punctuating his emphatic expressions created "inextinguishable laughter" among the men. It would be less of a trial for him to move forward than to sit still with those rifle balls coming thick and fast at his head.

Major Quinn was in command of the regiment, and that was a fact calculated to inspire confidence. He was not likely in any excitement to do some crazy thing. He seemed never to get excited. The lieutenant who temporarily "lost his head," figuratively speaking, in the fear that he would lose it literally, seemed that day the solitary exception.

From the right of the line Captain Jones was sent with his squadron, Companies A and D, across the fields to the west, where Powell had been persistently crowding the enemy back. Three distinct charges Powell had made, driving the enemy out of their earthworks on the hills, capturing the first prisoners, eighty in number, and two guns. Now he was working his way around Early's extreme left, attacking wherever there was a chance, creating an uneasiness that served to quicken the retreat that was soon to begin.

After a little the second squadron, Companies H and F, from the right of the regiment was sent in the same direction. The third squadron, B and C, did not have a commissioned officer present in the line. All that were in the field were doing staff duty—regimental, brigade and division. These companies were commanded by Orderly Sergeant Beach of Co. B. Major Quinn had been out in the front with Averell. Now he came back saying that there was a Confederate gun out in the field, supported by a body of cavalry, and Averell wanted a part of this regiment to capture that gun. He ordered the sergeant to take his two companies and report to the general. The order was promptly obeyed. There was warm work along the front line. Bullets were flying thickly about, and every few seconds a shell came plunging through. To all these the general seemed indifferent. He was intently watching the movements of the opposing lines, and the chances. Out in the open field was the gun with its support. The men of the squadron, ordered up to take that gun, gathered their reins, gripped their sabers, and fixed themselves firmly in their saddles. The impulse to rush forward for the gun was strong. But the general said, "Wait, wait; they are too many for you. Dismount your men and take them out along that stone wall and get a cross fire on them." Leaving as few as were necessary to hold the horses, the sergeant and the rest of the men made quick time in getting out along the wall which extended out to the right of the gun. Here, at short range, with their carbines they poured so hot a fire into the flank of the enemy that in less than a minute the supporting cavalry began to waver. Another mounted force from Averell's line was now starting forward on the charge. Seeing this force coming, the dismounted men jumped over the stone wall and ran at the top of their speed toward the gun. The supports, seeing both bodies coming upon them, the one mounted in front and the other dismounted on the left, fired their last shots, then broke and fled. The dismounted men were at the captured cannon as soon as the mounted men were, and exultingly drew it in by hand.

As the army closed in upon the enemy, the cavalry of Merritt and that of Averell, in almost a continuous line, presented a formidable array. There was still a body of cavalry, Fitz Hugh Lee's, between this line and Winchester. Soon, away off to the left, bugles were sounding the charge. Quickly the call was repeated and passed along toward the right. Then came up a long line of flashing sabers. A mile and more of horsemen moved forward out into the wide, open plain. Off to the right another mile and more of parts of a less continuous line were moving forward with increasing speed, aiming to get around the enemy's left. In all the annals of war a more inspiring sight was seldom seen than those thousands of splendid cavalry moving forward with a momentum that was irresistible. In attempting to withstand the onset Fitz Hugh Lee was wounded, and all the opposing forces were sent "whirling" through Winchester.

October 9, Early wrote to General Lee:

"Breckinridge was scarcely in position before our cavalry on the left was discovered coming back in great confusion followed by the enemy's, and Breckinridge's force was ordered to the left to repel this cavalry force, which had gotten in rear of my left, and this with the assistance of the artillery he succeeded in doing. But as soon as the firing was heard in the rear of our left flank, the infantry commenced falling back along the whole line, and it was very difficult to stop them. I succeeded, however, in stopping enough of them in the old rifle pits constructed by General Johnston to arrest the progress of the enemy's infantry, which commenced advancing again, when confusion in our ranks was discovered,

and we would still have won the day if our cavalry would have stopped the enemy's, but so overwhelming was the latter, and so demoralized was the larger part of ours, that no assistance was received from it.

The enemy's cavalry again charged around my left flank, which began to give way again, so that it was necessary for me to retire through the town."

This day's work is referred to in the following letter from General Averell:

"My recollections of regiments are like those of persons: there were no two alike, each had its distinguishing characteristics, and some remain well defined in memory while others are dimmed, but of none have I a stronger, clearer memory than the First New York Cavalry. Its chief characteristics were: It was always ready for duty, day or night; never complained; could camp anywhere; there was nothing heavy about its dashing cavalrymen and they possessed an irrepressible "go." One of the handsomest charges of cavalry against cavalry, I ever saw, was made by the First New York, on the nineteenth of September, '64, at Winchester. I remember when my division was sweeping across the broad fields toward Winchester, capturing the obstinate field works of the enemy on our right and swinging around upon the left flank and rear of Early's infantry, who had our infantry badly doubled back on its right flank, I held the First New York, then dwindled to a handful of three or four hundred men, in reserve. My line was so extended and impetuous in its advance, that a small, reliable reserve was necessary to use in the exigencies that were likely to arise. We were well across the field, carrying the little forts on the right by assault, and driving in the enemy's flank defense from behind their stone walls and corners, when a body of the enemy's cavalry appeared opposite my left in the open field, supporting a field piece which was opened upon my lines with a raking fire. They were three or four hundred strong and were in good order, steady and

resolute. The distance to them was not above five hundred yards, for the small-arm fire of their cavalry reached the ground on which we were moving and wounded men about me.

I called on the First New York to charge them, and I remember the keen interest with which I watched the operation. It was a fair field, but the enemy were favored with the gun. The numbers were as nearly equal as possible. I felt that the advantage of position was with the enemy on slightly elevated ground. The First New York rode in column steadily at a slow trot in the face of a small-arm fire which I could see was telling on their horses and men. It was a matter of three minutes from the time the order was given. I expected the enemy to move forward to meet the charge, and he did attempt to do so when it was too late.

The First New York took the charge at about two hundred yards and was upon him, and the field was swept back in that direction several hundred yards, when the First New York rallied in good order and the gun was ours. Others, however, claimed it and almost everything else on the field that day, even the taking of the forts on our extreme right, together with the guns captured in them. But the brave Captain Duncan of the Fourteenth Pennsylvania cavalry and others left their bodies there to attest the work of my division."

Indian Wars

Forsyth and the Rough Riders of Sixty-Eight

Adapted from Indian Fights and Fighters: The Soldier and the Sioux
by Cyrus Townsend Brady

Forsyth Versus Roman Nose

No one will question the sweeping assertion that the grittiest band of American fighters that history tells us of was that which defended the Alamo. But close on the heels of the gallant Travis and his dauntless comrades came "Sandy" Forsyth's original "Rough Riders," who immortalized themselves by their terrific fight on Beecher's Island on the Arickaree Fork of the Republican River, in Eastern Colorado, in the fall of 1868.

The contagion of the successful Indian attacks had spread all over the Central West. The Kansas Pacific was then building to Denver, and its advance was furiously resisted by the Indians. As early as 1866, at a council held at Fort Ellsworth, Roman Nose, head chief of the Cheyennes, made a speech full of insolent defiance.

"This is the first time," said the gigantic warrior, who was six feet three and magnificently proportioned, "that I have ever shaken the white man's hand in friendship. If the railway is continued I shall be his enemy forever."

There was no stopping the railway. Its progress was as irresistible as the movement of civilization itself. The Indians went on the warpath. The Cheyennes were led by their two principal chiefs, Black Kettle being the second.

Roman Nose stood six foot three inches tall, and towered giant-like above his companions; a grand head with strongly marked features, lighted by a pair of fierce black eyes; a large mouth with thin lips, through which gleamed rows of strong, white teeth; a Roman nose with dilated nostrils like those of a thoroughbred horse, first attracted attention, while a broad chest, with symmetrical limbs on which the muscles under the bronze of his skin stood out like twisted wire, were some of the points of this splendid animal. Clad in buckskin leggings and moccasins elaborately embroidered with beads and feathers, with a single eagle feather in his scalp-lock, and with that rarest of robes, a white buffalo, beautifully tanned and soft as cashmere, thrown over his naked shoulders, he stood forth, the war chief of the Cheyennes.

As fighters, these Indians are entitled to every admiration. As marauders, they merit nothing but censure. The Indians of the early days of the nation, when Pennsylvania and New York were border states, and across the Alleghenies lay the frontier, were cruel enough, as the chronicle of the times abundantly testify; but they were angels of light compared with the Sioux and Cheyennes, the Kiowas, Arapahoes and Comanches, and these in turn were almost admirable beside the Apache.

As patriots defending their country, they are not without certain definite claims to our respect. Recognizing the right of the aborigines to the soil, the government has yet arbitrarily abrogated that right at pleasure. At times the Indians have been regarded as independent nations, with which all differences were to be settled by treaty as between equals; and again, as a body of subjects whose affairs could be and

would be administered willy-nilly by the United States. Such vacilla-
tions are certain to result in trouble, especially as, needless to say, the
Indians invariably considered themselves as much independent nations
as England and France might consider themselves, in dealing with the
United States or with one another. And the Indians naturally claimed
and insisted that the territory where their fathers had roamed for cen-
turies belonged solely and wholly to them. They admitted no suzerain-
ty of any sort, either. And they held the petty force the government put
in the field in supreme contempt until they learned by bitter experience
the unlimited power of the United States.

The Cheyennes swept through Western Kansas like a devastating
storm. In one month, they cut off, killed, or captured eighty-four different settlers, including their wives and children. They swept the country bare. Again and again the different gangs of builders were wiped
out, but the railroad went on. General Sheridan finally took the field
in person, as usual with an inadequate force at his disposal. One of his
aides-de-camp was a young cavalry officer named George Alexander
Forsyth, commonly known to his friends as "Sandy" Forsyth. He had
entered the volunteer army in 1861 as a private of dragoons in a Chi-
cago company. A mere boy, he had come out a brigadier-general. In the
permanent establishment, he was a major in the Ninth Cavalry. Sheridan knew him. He was one of the two officers who made that magnificent ride with the great commander that saved the day at Winchester,
and it was due to his suggestion that Sheridan rode down the readjust-
ed lines before they made the return advance which decided the fate of
the battle. During all that mad gallop and hard fighting young Forsyth
rode with the General.

Forsyth was a fighter all through, and he wanted to get into the
field in command of some of the troops operating directly on the Indians in the campaign under consideration. No officer was willing to
surrender his command to Forsyth on the eve of active operations,
and there was no way, apparently, by which he could do anything until
Sheridan acceded to his importunities by authorizing him to raise a

company of scouts for the campaign. He was directed, if he could do so, to enlist fifty men, who, as there was no provision for the employment of scouts or civilian auxiliaries, were of necessity carried on the payrolls as quartermasters' employees for the magnificent sum of one dollar per day. They were to provide their own horses, but were allowed thirty cents a day for the use of them, and the horses were to be paid for by the government if they were "expended" during the campaign. They were equipped with saddle, bridle, haversack, canteen, blanket, knife, tin cup, Spencer repeating rifle, good for seven shots without reloading, six in the magazine, one in the barrel, and a heavy Colt's army revolver. There were no tents or other similar conveniences, and four mules constituted the baggage train. The force was intended to be strictly mobile, and it was. Each man carried on his person one hundred and forty rounds of ammunition for his rifle and thirty rounds for his revolver. The four mules carried the medical supplies and four thousand rounds of extra ammunition. Each officer and man took seven days' rations. What he could not carry on his person was loaded on the pack mules; scanty rations they were, too.

As soon as it was known that the troop was to be organized, Forsyth was overwhelmed with applications from men who wished to join it. He had the pick of the frontier to select from. He chose thirty men at Fort Harker and the remaining twenty from Fort Hayes. Undoubtedly they were the best men in the West for the purpose. To assist him, Lieutenant Frederick H. Beecher, of the Third Infantry, was detailed as second in command. Beecher was a young officer with a record. He had displayed peculiar heroism at the great battle of Gettysburg, where he had been so badly wounded that he was lame for the balance of his life. He was a nephew of the great Henry Ward Beecher and a worthy representative of the distinguished family whose name he bore. The surgeon of the party was Dr. John H. Mooers, a highly trained physician, who had come West in a spirit of restless adventure. He had settled at Hayes City and was familiar with the frontier. The guide of the party was Sharp Grover, one of the remarkable plainsmen of the time, regarded as the best scout in the government service. The first sergeant was W. H. H. McCall, formerly brigadier-general, United States Volunteers. McCall, in command of a Pennsylvania regiment, had been promoted for conspicuous gallantry on the field, when John B. Gordon made his magnificent dash out of Petersburg and attacked Fort Steadman.

The personnel of the troop was about equally divided between hunters and trappers and veterans of the Civil War, nearly all of whom had held commissions in either the Union or Confederate Army, for the command included men from both sides of Mason and Dixon's line. It was a hard-bitten, unruly group of fighters.

Forsyth was just the man for them. While he did not attempt to enforce the discipline of the Regular Army, he kept them regularly in hand. He took just five days to get his men and start on the march. They left Fort Wallace, the temporary terminus of the Kansas Pacific Railroad, in response to a telegram from Sheridan that the Indians were in force in the vicinity, and scouted the country for some six days, finally striking the Indian trail, which grew larger and better defined as they pursued it. Although it was evident that the Indians they were chasing greatly outnumbered them, they had come out for a fight and wanted one, so they pressed on. They got one, too.

The Island of Death

On the evening of the fifteenth of September, hot on the trail, now like a well-beaten road, they rode through a depression or a ravine, which gave entrance into a valley some two miles wide and about the same length. Through this valley ran a little river, the Arickaree. They encamped on the south bank of the river about four o'clock in the afternoon. The horses and men were weary with hard riding. Grazing was good. They were within striking distance of the Indians now. Forsyth believed there were too many of them to run away from such a small body as his troop of scouts. He was right. The Indians had retreated as far as they intended to.

The riverbed, which was bordered by wild plums, willows and alders, ran through the middle of the valley. The bed of the river was
about one hundred and forty yards wide. In the middle of it was an
island about twenty yards wide and sixty yards long. The gravelly upper
end of the island, which rose about two feet above the water level, was
covered with a thick growth of stunted bushes, principally alders and
willows; at the lower end, which sloped to the water's edge, there rose a
solitary cottonwood tree. There had been little rain for some time, and
this riverbed for the greater part of its width was dry and hard. For a
space of four or five yards on either side of the island there was water,
not over a foot deep, languidly washing the graveled shores. When the
riverbed was full the island probably was overflowed. Such islands form
from time to time, and are washed away as quickly as they develop. The
banks of the riverbed on either side commanded the island.

The simple preparations for the camp of that body of men were
soon made. As night fell they rolled themselves in their blankets, with
the exception of the sentries, and went to sleep with the careless indifference of veterans under such circumstances.

Forsyth, however, as became a captain, was not so careless or so
reckless as his men. They were alone in the heart of the Indian country,
in close proximity to an overwhelming force, and liable to attack at
any moment. He knew that their movements had been observed by the
Indians during the past few days. Therefore, the young commander was
on the alert throughout the night, visiting the outposts from time to
time to see that careful watch was kept.

Just as the first streaks of dawn began to "lace the severing clouds,"
he happened to be standing by the sentry farthest from the camp. Sil-
houetted against the skyline they saw the feathered head of an Indian.
For Forsyth to fire at him was the work of an instant. At the same time
a party which had crept nearer to the picket line unobserved dashed
boldly at the horses, and resorting to the usual devices with bells, horns,

hideous yells, and waving buffalo robes, attempted to stampede the herd.

Men like those scouts under such circumstances slept with their boots on. The first shot called them into instant action. They ran instinctively to the picket line. A sharp fire, and the Indians were driven off at once. Only the pack mules got away. No pursuit was attempted, of course. Orders were given for the men to saddle their horses and stand by them. In a few moments, the command was drawn up in line, each man standing by his horse's head, bridle reins through his left arm, his rifle grasped in his right hand ready! Scarcely had the company been thus assembled when Grover caught Forsyth's arm and pointed down the valley.

"My God!" he cried, "look at the Injuns!"

In front of them, on the right of them, in the rear of them, the hills and valleys on both sides of the river seemed suddenly to be alive with Indians; as quick a transformation from a scene of peaceful quiet to a valley filled with an armed force.

The way to the left, by which they had entered the valley, was still open. Forsyth could have made a running fight for it and dashed for the gorge through which he had entered the valley. There were, apparently, no Indians barring the way in that direction. But Forsyth realized that for him to retreat would mean the destruction of his command, that the Indians had in all probability purposely left him that way of escape, and if he tried it he would be ambushed in the defile and slain. That was just what they wanted him to do, it was evident. That was why he did not attempt it. He was cornered, but he was not beaten, and he did not think he could be. Besides, he had come for that fight, and that fight he was bound to have.

Whatever he was to do he must do quickly. There was no place to which he could go save the island. It was not much of a place at best, but it was the one strategic point presented by the situation. Pouring a heavy fire into the Indians, Forsyth directed his men to take possession of the island under cover of the smoke. In the movement, everything had to be abandoned, including the medical stores and rations, but the precious ammunition that must be secured at all hazards. Protected by a squad of expert riflemen on the riverbank, who presently joined them, the scouts reached the island in safety, tied their horses to the bushes around the edge of it, and in the intervals of fighting set to work digging rifle pits covering an ellipse twenty by forty yards, one pit for each man, with which to defend the upper and higher part of the island. They had nothing to dig with except tin cups, tin plates, and their Bowie knives, but there was no lingering or hesitation about it.

The chief of the Indian force, which was made up of Northern Cheyennes, Oglala and Brule Sioux, with a few Arapahoes and a number of Dog Soldiers, was the famous Roman Nose, an enemy to be feared indeed. He was filled with disgust and indignation at the failure of his men to occupy the island, the strategic importance of which he at once detected. It is believed that orders to seize the island had been given, but for some reason they had not been obeyed; and to this oversight or failure was due the ultimate safety of Forsyth's men. It was not safe to neglect the smallest point in fighting with a soldier like Forsyth.

With more military skill than they had ever displayed before, the Indians deliberately made preparations for battle. The force at the disposal of Roman Nose was something less than one thousand warriors. They were accompanied by their squaws and children. The latter took position on the bluffs on the east bank of the river, just out of range, where they could see the whole affair. Like the ladies of the ancient tournaments, they were eager to witness the fighting and welcome the victors, who, for they never doubted the outcome, were certain to be their own.

Roman Nose next lined the banks of the river on both sides with dismounted riflemen, skillfully using such concealment as the ground afforded. The banks were slightly higher than the island, and the Indians had a plunging fire upon the little party. The riflemen on the banks opened fire at once. A storm of bullets was poured upon the devoted band on the island. The scouts, husbanding their ammunition, slowly and deliberately replied, endeavoring, with some success, to make every shot tell. As one man said, they reckoned "every cartridge was wuth at least one Injun." The horses of the troop, having no protection, received the brunt of the first fire. They fell rapidly, and their carcasses rising in front of the rifle pits afforded added protection to the soldiers. There must have been a renegade white man among the savages, for in a lull of the firing the men on the island heard a voice announce in perfect English, "There goes the last of their horses, anyway." Besides this, from time to time, the notes of an artillery bugle were heard from the shore. The casualties had not been serious while the horses stood, but as soon as they were all down the men began to suffer.

During this time, Forsyth had been walking about in the little circle of defenders encouraging his men. He was met on all sides with insistent demands that he lay down and take cover, and, the firing becoming hotter, he at last complied. The rifle pit which Surgeon Mooers had made was a little wider than that of the other men, and as it was a good place from which to direct the fighting, at the doctor's suggestion some of the scouts scooped it out to make it a little larger, and Forsyth lay down by him.

The fire of the Indians had been increasing. Several scouts were killed, more mortally wounded, and some slightly wounded. Doctor Mooers was hit in the forehead and mortally wounded. He lingered for three days, saying but one intelligent word during the whole period. Although he was blind and speechless, his motions sometimes indicated that he knew where he was. He would frequently reach out his foot and touch Forsyth. A bullet struck Forsyth in the right thigh, and glancing upwards bedded itself in the flesh, causing excruciating pain. He suffered exquisite anguish, but his present sufferings were just beginning, for a second bullet struck him in the leg, between the knee and ankle, and smashed the bone, and a third glanced across his forehead, slightly fracturing his skull and giving him a splitting headache, although he had no time to attend to it then.

The Charge of the Five Hundred

During all this time, Roman Nose and his horsemen had withdrawn around the bend up the river, which screened them from the island. At this juncture, they appeared in full force, trotting up the bed of the river in open order in eight ranks of about sixty front. Ahead of them, on a magnificent chestnut horse, trotted Roman Nose. The warriors were hideously painted, and all were naked except for moccasins and cartridge belts. Eagle feathers were stuck in their long hair, and many of them wore gorgeous feather war bonnets. They sat their horses without saddles or stirrups, some of them having lariats twisted around the horses' bellies. Roman Nose wore a magnificent war bonnet of feathers streaming behind him in the wind and surmounted by two buffalo-horns; around his waist he had tied an officer's brilliant scarlet silk sash, which had been presented to him at the Fort Ellsworth conference. The sunlight illumined the bronze body of this savage Hercules, exhibiting the magnificent proportions of the man.

As the Indian cavalry appeared around the bend, the fire upon the island from the banks redoubled in intensity. Forsyth instantly divined that Roman Nose was about to attempt to ride him down. He also realized that, so soon as the horses were upon him, the rifle fire from the bank would of necessity be stopped. His order to his men was to cease firing, therefore; to load the magazines of their rifles, charge their revolvers, and wait until he gave the order to fire. The rifles of the dead and those of the party too severely wounded to use them were distributed among those scouts yet unharmed. Some of the wounded insisted upon fighting. Forsyth propped himself up in his rifle pit, his back and shoulders resting against the pile of earth, his rifle and revolver in hand. He could see his own men, and also the Indians coming up the river.

Presently, shouting their war songs, at a wild pealed whoop from their chief, the Indian horsemen broke into a gallop, Roman Nose leading the advance, shaking his heavy Spencer rifle in the air as if it had been a reed. There was a last burst of rifle fire from the banks, and the rattle of musketry was displaced by the war songs of the Indians and the yells of the squaws and children on the slopes of the hills. As the smoke drifted away on that sunny September morning, they saw the Indians almost upon them. In spite of his terrible wounds Forsyth was thoroughly in command. Waiting until the tactical moment when the Indians were but fifty yards away and coming at a terrific speed, he raised himself on his hands to a sitting position and cried, "Now!"

The men rose to their knees, brought their guns to their shoulders, and poured a volley right into the face of the furious advance. An instant later, with another cartridge in the barrel they delivered a second volley. Horses and men went down in every direction; but, like the magnificent warriors they were, the Indians closed up and came sweeping down. The third volley was poured into them. Still they came. The war songs had ceased by this time, but in undaunted spirit, still pealing his war cry above the crashing of the bullets, at the head of his band, with his magnificent determination unshaken, Roman Nose led such a ride as no Indian ever attempted before or since. And still those quiet, cool men continued to pump bullets into the horde. At the fourth volley the medicine man on the left of the line and the second in command went down. The Indians hesitated at this reverse, but swinging his rifle high in the air in battle frenzy, the great war chief rallied them, and they once more advanced. The fifth volley staggered them still more. Great gaps were opened in their ranks. Horses and men fell dead, but the impetus was so great, and the courage and example of their leader so splendid, that the survivors came on unchecked. The sixth volley did the work. Just as he was about to leap on the island, Roman Nose and his horse were both shot to pieces. The force of the charge, however, was so great that the line was not yet entirely broken. The horsemen were within a few feet of the scouts, when the seventh volley was poured into their very faces. As a gigantic wave meets a sharply jutting rock and is parted harmlessly on either side of it, so was that charge divided, the Indians swinging themselves to the sides of their horses as they swept down the length of the island.

The scouts sprang to their feet at this juncture, and almost at contact range jammed their revolver shots at the disorganized masses. The Indians fled precipitately to the banks on either side, and the yelling of the war chants of the squaws and children changed into wails of anguish and despair, as they marked the death of Roman Nose and the horrible slaughter of his followers.

It was a most magnificent charge, and one which for splendid daring and reckless heroism would have done credit to the best troops of any nation in the world. And magnificently had it been met.

As soon as the Indian horsemen withdrew, baffled and furious, a rifle fire opened once more from the banks. Lieutenant Beecher, who had heroically performed his part in the defense, crawled over to Forsyth and said:

"I have my death wound, General. I am shot in the side and dying." He said the words quietly and simply, as if his communication was utterly commonplace, then stretched himself out by his wounded commander, lying with his face upon his arm.

"No, Beecher, no," said Forsyth, out of his own anguish; "it cannot be as bad as that."

"Yes," said the young officer, "good night."

There was nothing to be done for him. Forsyth heard him whisper a word or two of his mother, and then delirium supervened. By evening he was dead. In memory of the brave young officer, they called the place where he had died Beecher's Island.

At two o'clock in the afternoon a second charge of horse was assayed in much the same way as the first had been delivered; but there was no longer a great war chief in command, and this time the Indians broke at one hundred yards from the island. At six o'clock at night they made a final attempt. The whole party, horse and foot, in a solid mass rushed from all sides upon the island. They came forward, yelling and firing, but they were met with so severe a fire from the rifle pits that, although some of them actually reached the foot of the island, they could not maintain their position, and were driven back with frightful loss. The men on the island deliberately picked off Indian after Indian as they came, so that the dry river ran with blood. The place was a very hell to the Indians. They withdrew at last, baffled, crushed, beaten.

With nightfall, the men on the island could take account of the situation. Two officers and four men were dead or dying, one officer and eight men were so severely wounded that their condition was critical. Eight men were less severely wounded, making twenty-three casualties out of fifty-one officers and men. There were no rations, but thank God there was an abundance of water. They could get it easily by digging in the sandy surface of the island. They could subsist, if necessary, on strips of meat cut from the bodies of the horses. The most serious lack was of medical attention. The doctor lying unconscious, the wounded were forced to get along with the unskilled care of their comrades, and with water, and rags torn from clothing for dressings. Little could be done for them. The day had been frightfully hot, but, fortunately, a heavy rain fell in the night, which somewhat refreshed them. The rifle pits were deepened and made continuous by piling saddles and equipment, and by further digging in the interspaces.

One of the curious Indian superstitions, which has often served the white man against whom he has fought to good purpose, is that when a man is killed in the dark he must pass all eternity in darkness. Consequently, he rarely ever attacks at night. Forsyth's party felt reasonably secure from any further attack, notwithstanding which, they kept watch.

The Siege of the Island

As soon as darkness settled down, volunteers were called for to carry the news of their predicament to Fort Wallace, one hundred miles away. Every man able to travel offered himself for the perilous journey. Forsyth selected Trudeau and Stillwell. Trudeau was a veteran hunter, Stillwell a youngster only nineteen years of age, although he already gave promise of the fame as a scout which he afterwards acquired. To them he gave the only map he possessed. They were to ask the commander of Fort Wallace to come to his assistance. As soon as the two brave scouts had left, everyone realized that a long wait would be entailed upon the little band, if, indeed, it was not overwhelmed meanwhile, before any relieving force could reach the island. And there were grave doubts as to whether, in any event, Trudeau and Stillwell could get through the Indians. It was not a pleasant night they spent, therefore, although they were busy strengthening the defenses, and nobody got any sleep.

Early the next morning the Indians again made their appearance. They had hoped that Forsyth and his men would have endeavored to retreat during the night, in which event they would have followed the trail and speedily annihilated the whole command. But Forsyth was too good a soldier to leave the position he had chosen.

During the fighting of the day before, he had asked Grover his opinion as to whether the Indians could deliver any more formidable attack than the one which had resulted in the death of Roman Nose, and Grover, who had had large experience, assured him that they had done the best they could, and indeed better than he or any other scout had ever seen or heard of in any Indian warfare. Forsyth was satisfied, therefore, that they could maintain the position, at least until they starved.

The Indians were quickly apprised, by a volley which killed at least one man, that the defenders of the island were still there. The place was closely invested, and although the Indians made several attempts to approach it under a white flag, they were forced back by the accurate fire of the scouts, and compelled to keep their distance. It was very hot. The sufferings of the wounded were something frightful. The Indians were having troubles of their own, too. All night and all day the defenders could hear the beating of the tom-toms or drums and the mournful death songs and wails of the women over the bodies of the slain, all but three of whom had been removed during the night. These three were lying so near the rifle pits that the Indians did not dare to approach near enough to get them. The three dead men had actually gained the shore of the island before they had been killed.

The command on the island had plenty to eat, such as it was. There was horse and mule meat in abundance. They ate it raw, when they got hungry enough. Water was plentiful. All they had to do was to dig the rifle pits a little deeper, and it came forth in great quantities. It was weary waiting, but there was nothing else to do. They dared not relax their vigilance a moment. The next night, the second, Forsyth dispatched two more scouts, fearing the first two might not have got through, thus seeking to "make assurance double sure." This pair was not so successful as the first. They came back about three o'clock in the morning, having been unable to pass the Indians, for every outlet was heavily guarded.

The third day the Indian women and children were observed withdrawing from the vicinity. This cheered the men greatly, as it was a sign that the Indians intended to abandon the siege. The warriors still remained, however, and any incautious exposure was a signal for a volley. That night two more men were dispatched with an urgent appeal, and these two succeeded in getting through. They bore this message:

Sept. 19, 1868.
To COLONEL BANKHEAD, or Commanding Officer,
Fort Wallace:

I sent you two messengers on the night of the seventeenth inst., informing you of my critical condition. I tried to send two more last night, but they did not succeed in passing the Indian pickets, and returned. If the others have not arrived, then hasten at once to my assistance.

I have eight badly wounded and ten slightly wounded men to take in. . . . Lieutenant Beecher is dead, and Acting Assistant Surgeon Mooers probably cannot live the night out. He was hit in the head Thursday, and has spoken but one rational word since. I am wounded in two places in the right thigh, and my left leg is broken below the knee.

I am on a little island, and have still plenty of ammunition left. We are living on mule and horsemeat, and are entirely out of rations. If it was not for so many wounded, I would come in, and take the chances of whipping them if attacked. They are evidently sick of their bargain. . . . I can hold out for six days longer if absolutely necessary, but please lose no time.

P.S. My surgeon having been mortally wounded, none of my wounded have had their wounds dressed yet, so please bring out a surgeon with you.

The fourth day passed like the preceding, the squaws all gone, the Indians still watchful. The wound in Forsyth's leg had become excruciatingly painful, and he begged some of the men to cut out the bullet. But they discovered that it had lodged near the femoral artery, and fearful lest they should cut the artery and the young commander should bleed to death, they positively refused. In desperation, Forsyth cut it out himself. He had his razor in his saddlebags and, while two men pressed the flesh back, he performed the operation successfully, to his immediate relief.

The fifth day the mule and horsemeat became putrid and therefore unfit to eat. An unlucky coyote wandered over to the island, however, and one of the men was fortunate enough to shoot him. Small though he was, he was a welcome addition to their larder, for he was fresh. There was but little skirmishing on the fifth day, and the place appeared to be deserted. Forsyth had half a dozen of his men raise him on a blanket above the level of the rifle beds so that he might survey the scene himself. Not all the Indians were gone, for a sudden fusillade burst out from the bank. One of the men let go the corner of the blanket which he held while the others were easing Forsyth down, and he fell upon his wounded leg with so much force that the bone protruded through the flesh. He records that he used some severe language to that scout.

On the sixth day Forsyth assembled his men about him, and told them that those who were well enough to leave the island would better do so and make for Fort Wallace; that it was more than possible that none of the messengers had succeeded in getting through; that the men had stood by him heroically, and that they would all starve to death where they were unless relief should come; and that they were entitled to a chance for their lives. He believed the Indians, who had at last disappeared, had received such a severe lesson that they would not attack again, and that if the men were circumspect they could get through to Fort Wallace in safety. The wounded must be left to take care of themselves and take the chances of escape from the island. The proposition was received in surprised silence for a few moments, and then there was a simultaneous shout of refusal from every man: "Never! We'll stand by you." McCall, the first sergeant and Forsyth's right-hand man since Beecher had been killed, shouted out emphatically: "We've fought together, and, by Heaven, if need be, we'll die together."

They could not carry the wounded; they would not abandon them. Remember these men were not regular soldiers. They were simply a company of scouts, more or less loosely bound together, but, as McCall had pointed out, they were tied to one another by something stronger than discipline. Not a man left the island, although it would have been easy for the unwounded to do so, and possibly they might have escaped in safety.

For two more days, they stood it out. There was no fighting during this time, but the presence of an Indian *vedette* indicated that they were under observation.

They gathered some wild plums and made some jelly for the wounded; but no game came their way, and there was little for them to do but draw in their belts a little tighter and go hungry, or, better, go hungrier. On the morning of the ninth day, one of the men on watch suddenly sprang to his feet, shouting:

"There are moving men on the hills." Everybody who could stand was up in an instant, and Grover, the keen-eyed scout, shouted triumphantly:

"By the God above us, there's an ambulance!" They were rescued at last.

The Journey of the Scouts and the Rescue of Forsyth

Trudeau and Stillwell, the first pair of scouts dispatched by Forsyth with the story of his desperate situation on Beecher's Island, left their commander about midnight on the evening of the first day of the attack. The Indians had withdrawn from the immediate vicinity of the river and were resting quietly in the camps on either side, although there were a number of warriors watching the island. The men bade a hasty goodbye to their comrades, received their captain's final instructions, and with beating hearts stole away on their desperate errand.

They neglected no precaution that experience could dictate. They took off their boots, tied them together by the straps, slung them around their necks, and walked backward down the bed of the river in their stocking feet, so that, if the Indians by any chance stumbled upon their trail the next morning, it would appear to have been made by moccasined feet and perhaps escape attention, especially as the tracks would point toward the island instead of away from it. Further to disguise themselves, they wrapped themselves in blankets, which they endeavored to wear as the Indians did.

They proceeded with the most fearsome caution. Such was the circumspection with which they moved and the care necessary because of the watchfulness of the foe, who might be heard from time to time moving about on the banks, that by daylight they had progressed but two miles. During most of the time after leaving the riverbed they had crawled on their hands and knees. Before sunrise they were forced to seek such concealment as they could find in a washout, a dry ravine, within sight and sound of the Indian camps. Providence certainly protected them, for if any of the Indians had happened to wander in their direction there was nothing to prevent their discovery; and if the Indians had stumbled upon their hiding place it would have been all up with them. Death by torture would have been inevitable if they were taken alive, and the only way to prevent that would be suicide. They had determined upon that. They had pledged each other to fight until the last cartridge, and to save that for themselves. They had nothing to eat and nothing to drink.

The sun beat down upon them fiercely all the long day. After their experience of the one before, it was a day calculated to break down the strongest of men. They bore up under the strain, however, as best they could, and when darkness came they started out once more.

This night there was no necessity for so much caution and they made better progress, although they saw and successfully avoided several parties of Indians. When the day broke, they were forced to conceal themselves again. The country was covered with wandering war parties, and it was not yet safe to travel by daylight. This day they hid themselves under the high banks of a river. Again, they were fortunate in remaining unobserved, although several times bands of warriors passed near them. They traveled all the third night, making great progress. Morning found them on an open plain with no place to hide in but a buffalo wallow, a dry alkali mud-hole which had been much frequented in the wet season by buffalo, which afforded scanty cover at best.

During this day, a large party of scouting Indians halted within one hundred feet of the wallow. Simultaneously with their arrival a wandering rattlesnake made his appearance in front of the two scouts, who were hugging the earth and expecting every minute to be discovered. The rattlesnake in his way was as deadly as the Indians. The scouts could have killed him easily had it not been for the proximity of the Cheyennes. To make the slightest movement would call attention to their hiding place. Indeed, the sinister rattle of the venomous snake before he struck would probably attract the notice of the alert Indians. Between the savage reptile and the savage men the scouts were in a frightful predicament, which young Stillwell, a lad of amazing resourcefulness, instantly and effectually solved. He was chewing tobacco at the time, and as the snake drew near him and made ready to strike, he completely routed him by spitting tobacco juice in his mouth and eyes and all over his head. The rattlesnake fled; he could not stand such a dose. The Indians presently moved on, having noticed nothing, and so ended perhaps the most terrible half hour the two men had ever experienced.

They started early on the evening of the fourth night, and this time made remarkable progress. Toward morning, however, Trudeau all but broke down. The brunt of the whole adventure thereupon fell on Stillwell. He encouraged his older companion, helped him along as best he could, and finally, late at night, they reached Fort Wallace and told their tale. Instantly all was excitement in the post. Captain and Brevet Lieutenant-Colonel Louis H. Carpenter, with seventy men of Troop H, of the Tenth Cavalry (a negro regiment), with Lieutenants Banzhaf and Orleman, Doctor Fitzgerald and seventeen scouts, with thirteen wagons and an ambulance, had been sent out from the post the day before with orders to make a camp on the Denver road, about sixty miles from the fort. From there he was to scout in every direction, keep off the Indians, and protect trains.

At eleven o'clock at night a courier was dispatched to Carpenter with the following order:

Headquarters, Fort Wallace, Kansas,
September 22, 1868, 11:00 p.m.
Brevet Lieut. Colonel L. H. CARPENTER, 10th U. S. Cavalry.

Colonel:

The Commanding Officer directs you to proceed at once to a point on the "Dry Fork of the Republican," about seventy-five or eighty miles north, northwest from this point, thirty or forty miles west by a little south from the forks of the Republic, with all possible dispatch.

Two scouts from Colonel Forsyth's command arrived here this evening and bring word that he (Forsyth) was attacked on the morning of Thursday last by an overwhelming force of Indians (seven hundred), who killed all the animals, broke Colonel Forsyth's left leg with a rifle ball, severely wounding him in the groin, wounded Doctor Mooers in the head, and wounded Lieutenant Beecher in several places. His back is supposed to be broken. Two men of the command were killed and eighteen or twenty wounded.

The men bringing the word crawled on hands and knees two miles, and then traveled only by night on account of the Indians, whom they saw daily.

Forsyth's men were entrenched in the dry bed of the creek with a well in the trench, but had only horseflesh to eat and only sixty rounds of ammunition.

General Sheridan orders that the greatest dispatch be used and every means employed to succor Forsyth at once. Colonel Bradley with six companies is now supposed by General Sheridan to be at the forks of the Republic.

Colonel Bankhead will leave here in one hour with one hundred men and two mountain howitzers.

Bring all your scouts with you.

Order Doctor Fitzgerald at once to this post, to replace Doctor Turner, who accompanies Colonel Bankhead for the purpose of dressing the wounded of Forsyth's party.

I am, Colonel, very respectfully your obedient servant,

HUGH JOHNSON,
1st Lieutenant Fifth Infantry. Acting Post Adjutant.

One hour afterward Bankhead himself, with one hundred men and two howitzers and the surgeon, started for the relief of Forsyth. With Bankhead went the undaunted Stillwell as guide. Trudeau had suffered so much during the perilous journey that he was unable to accompany the relief party, and he soon afterward died from the hardships and excitement of the horrible days he had passed through.

Buffalo Soldiers to the Rescue

Carpenter had bivouacked on the evening of September 22 at Cheyenne Wells, about thirty-five miles from Fort Wallace. He had broken camp early in the morning and had marched some ten miles, when, from a high point on a divide he had reached, which permitted a full view of the Rocky Mountains from Pike's to Long's Peaks, he observed a horseman galloping frantically toward them. He was the courier dispatched by Colonel Bankhead. Carpenter was a splendid soldier. He had received no less than four brevets for gallantry during the Civil War. He had been on Sheridan's staff with Forsyth, and the two were bosom friends. No task could have been more congenial to him than this attempt at rescue.

He communicated the situation of their white comrades to his black troopers, and their officers crowded close about him. The orders were received with exultant cheers. The regiment had been raised since the war, and had not yet had a chance to prove its mettle. There were no veterans among them, and Carpenter and the other officers had been obliged to build the regiment from the ground up. Now was an opportunity to show what they could do. Carpenter had been trained to obey orders to the letter. In this instance, he determined to disobey the command regarding Doctor Fitzgerald. It appeared to him that Bankhead had little hope that he (Carpenter) would find Forsyth, for he had sent him no guide; but Carpenter perceived that if he did find Forsyth—and he intended to find him—the conditions would be such that the services of a physician would be vitally necessary. He therefore retained the doctor. He also retained the wagon train, having no other way of carrying necessary supplies. For one reason, if he had detached a guard for the train, it would have weakened his force so greatly as to have made it inadequate to the enterprise. The mules were strong and fresh, and he decided to keep the wagons with him. The pace was to be a fast one, and he instructed the wagon masters that, if any of the mule teams gave out, they should be shot and, if necessary, the wagon should be abandoned.

There was no one in his command, he found, who had ever been in that territory. Indeed, it is probable that, save Forsyth's men, no white men had ever penetrated that section of the country before. The map that Carpenter had was very defective. He studied over the matter a few moments, and then led his command toward the place where he supposed Forsyth to be.

They advanced at a fast trot, with intervals of walking, and when they camped at night near some water holes they had covered nearly forty-five miles. The mules, under the indefatigable and profane stimulus of their drivers, had kept up with the rest. As soon as it was dawn the next day they started once more, and, after a twenty-mile ride, arrived at the dry bed of a river.

Whether this was the fork of the Republican, on which Forsyth was besieged, no one could tell. It happens that the Republican has three forks: a north fork, the Arickaree, and the south or dry fork. Carpenter was afraid to leave the fork he had found without satisfying himself that Forsyth was not there, so he concluded to scout up the river for some fifteen or eighteen miles. Finding nothing, he then turned northward again until he came to a stream flowing through a wide, grass-covered valley surrounded by high hills. As they entered the valley they came across a very large, fresh Indian trail. The scouts estimated that at least two thousand ponies had passed along the trail within a few hours. Various other signs showed a large village had moved down the trail.

They had traveled over forty miles this second day, and were apprehensive that the Indians, being so close to them, might attack them. It was nearly evening. A spot well adapted for defense was chosen near the water, the wagons were corralled, and preparations made for a stout resistance in case of an attack. While the men were making camp, Carpenter with a small escort rode to the top of one of the high hills bordering the valley. He could see for miles, but discovered no Indians nor any other living object in any direction. In front of them, however, on the top of another hill, were a number of scaffolds, each one bearing a human body. The Cheyenne method of burial was instantly recognized. A nearer look developed that the scaffolds had been recently erected. Five of them were examined, and in each case the body contained was that of a Cheyenne warrior, who had been killed by a gunshot wound. This was proof positive that they were some of the Indians who had been fighting against Forsyth.

While this was going on, one of the troopers noticed something white in a ravine on the opposite side of the valley. They galloped over to it, and found it to be an elaborate and beautiful tepee or wigwam, made out of freshly tanned white buffalo skins. The colonel dismounted, opened the tepee, and entered. There, upon a brush heap, lay a human figure wrapped in buffalo robes.

When the robes were taken away the body of a splendid specimen of Indian manhood was disclosed. "He lay like a warrior taking his rest, with his martial cloak around him." His stern and royal look, the iron majesty of his features, even though composed in death, revealed at once a native chieftain. In his breast was a great, gaping wound, which had pierced his heart. He lay in his war-gear, with his weapons and other personal property close at hand. After the examination, they re-covered him and left him undisturbed. Then they went back to the camp.

The corral was watchfully guarded during the night, but no one appeared to molest them. It was decided to follow the Indian trail at daylight, as it would probably lead to the site of Forsyth's fight. Early the next morning, while they were packing up, they saw some horsemen coming over the hills to the south of them. They were white men, led by a scout named Donovan. Two more men had been dispatched by Forsyth from the island on the third night of the siege, and being unobserved by the Indians, they had made their way to Fort Wallace. When they arrived there they found that Colonel Bankhead had already gone; whereupon Donovan had assembled five bold spirits and had immediately started out on the return journey. Fortunately for Carpenter, Donovan had struck the latter's trail, and had followed it to the camp.

Carpenter thereupon took thirty of his best mounted troopers and the ambulance loaded with hard-tack, coffee, and bacon, and set out on a gallop in the direction in which they supposed the island lay. Banzhaf was left in command of the rest, with orders to come on as fast as he could.

Carpenter went forward at a rapid gallop, and after traveling eighteen miles, while it was yet early in the morning, came to a spur of land from which he had a view of the surrounding country for miles. As he checked his horse on the brink, he saw to the right of him a valley through which meandered a narrow silver stream.

In the center of the valley there was an island. From it rose a solitary cottonwood. Men could be seen moving about the place. Donovan recognized it instantly. The horses of the detachment were put to a run, and the whole party galloped down the valley toward the island.

The scouts swarmed across the river with cries of joy, and welcomed the soldiers. The faithful mules dragged the ambulance close behind. There was food for everybody. Carpenter was struck with the wolfish look on the faces of the hungry men as they crowded around the ambulance. Later one of them brought him a piece of mule or horsemeat which was to have been served for dinner that day, if the rescuers had not appeared. Carpenter could not endure even the odor of it.

Galloping across the river bed, the first to enter the rifle pits on the island was Carpenter. There, on the ground before him, lay Forsyth. And what do you suppose he was doing? He was reading a novel! Someone had found, in an empty saddlebag, an old copy of *Oliver Twist*. Forsyth was afraid to trust himself. He was fearful that he would break down. He did not dare look at Carpenter or express his feelings. Therefore, he made a pretense of being absorbed in his book.

The black cavalry had arrived in the very nick of time. Forsyth was in a burning fever. Blood poisoning had set in, and his wounds were in a frightful condition. Another day and it would have been too late. Everything was gone from him but his indomitable resolution. Many others were in like circumstances. It was well that Carpenter had brought his surgeon with him, for his services were sadly needed. The men were taken off the island, moved half a mile away from the terrible stench arising from the dead animals; the wagon train came up, camps were made, the dead were buried on the island they had immortalized with their valor, and everything possible done for the comfort of the living by their negro comrades.

The doctor wanted to amputate Forsyth's leg, but he protested, so that the amputation was not performed, and the leg was finally saved to its owner. One of the scouts, named Farley, however, was so desperately wounded that amputation had to be resorted to. The doctor performed the operation, assisted by Carpenter. A military commander in the field has to do a great many things.

The next day Bankhead made his appearance with his detachment. He had marched to the forks of the river and followed the Arickaree fork to the place. He was accompanied by two troops of the Second Cavalry, picked up on the way. He did not find fault with Carpenter for his disobedience in retaining Doctor Fitzgerald. On the contrary, such was his delight at the rescue that he fairly hugged his gallant subordinate.

As soon as it was possible, the survivors were taken back to Fort Wallace. Forsyth and the more severely wounded were carried in the ambulance. It took four days to reach the fort. Their progress was one long torture, in spite of every care that could be bestowed upon them. There was no road, and while the drivers chose the best spots on the prairie, there was, nevertheless, an awful amount of jolting and bumping.

Forsyth was brevetted a brigadier-general in the Regular Army for his conduct in this action. This was some compensation for two years of subsequent suffering until his wounds finally healed.

The End of Roman Nose

On the way back, the men stopped at the white tepee in the lonely valley. Grover and McCall rode over to the spot with the officers and examined the body of the chieftain. They instantly identified him as Roman Nose. With a touch of sentiment unusual in frontiersmen they respected his grave, and for the sake of his valor allowed him to sleep on undisturbed. His arms and equipment, however, were considered legitimate spoils of war, and were taken from him. It was a sad end, indeed, to all his splendid courage and glorious defiance of his white foemen.

The loss of the Indians in the several attacks was never definitely ascertained. They admitted to seventy-five killed outright and over two hundred seriously wounded, but it is certain that their total losses were much greater. The fighting was of the closest and fiercest description, and the Indians were under the fire of one of the most expert bodies of marksmen on the plains at half pistol-shot distance in the unique and celebrated battle. The whole action is almost unparalleled in the history of our Indian wars, both for the thrilling and gallant cavalry charge of the Indians and the desperate valor of Forsyth and his scouts.

A Few Words About Forsyth's Men

A man named Farley had fought through the action with a severe bullet wound in the shoulder, which he never mentioned until nightfall; his wound was mortal, but he lay on his side and fought through the whole of the long first day until he died. Another man named Harrington was struck in the forehead by an arrow. He pulled out the shaft, but the head remained imbedded in the bone. An Indian bullet struck him a glancing blow in the forehead and neatly extricated the arrow; rough surgery, to be sure, but it served. Harrington tied a rag around his head, and kept his place during the whole three days of fighting.

When they first reached the island one of the men cried out, "Don't let's stay here and be shot down like dogs! Will any man try for the opposite bank with me?" Forsyth, revolver in hand, stopped that effort by threatening to shoot any man who attempted to leave the island. In all the party, there was but one coward. In looks and demeanor he was the most promising of the company—a splendid specimen of manhood apparently. To everybody's surprise, after one shot he hugged the earth in his rifle pit and positively refused to do anything, in spite of orders, pleadings, jeers, and curses. He left the troop immediately on its arrival at Fort Wallace.

Per contra, one of the bravest—where all but one were heroes— was a little, eighteen-year old Jewish boy, who had begged to be enlisted and allowed to go along. He had been the butt of the command, yet he proved himself a very paladin of courage and efficiency when the fighting began.

The Buffalo Soldiers Fight at Beaver Creek
By L. H. Carpenter

While on the forced march to relieve the party of scouts with Colonel George A. Forsyth, surrounded by Indians on the Arickaree fork of the Republican River, the troops under my command discovered a large trail of the Indians who had been engaged in that fight on the south fork of the Republican. The scouts discovered that this trail left the valley of the stream a short distance below and struck across country in the direction of the Beaver Creek. After the relief of Forsyth, on my return to Fort Wallace with the survivors and wounded, a report was made to General Sheridan, then to the east of Fort Hayes, Kansas, of the probable whereabouts of the Indians; and the Fifth Cavalry, which had just arrived from the East by rail, was disembarked between Hayes and Wallace and ordered to move north under Major Royall, and strike the savages, if possible, on the Beaver. A day or two after the Fifth had left, Brevet-Major-General Eugene A. Carr reported for duty to General Sheridan. Carr had been a general officer of volunteers during the Civil War with an excellent record, and now reverted to his rank in the regulars of Major in the Fifth Cavalry.

Sheridan was anxious to have Carr join his regiment because of his experience with Indians and his general reputation, and therefore sent him to Fort Wallace with orders to have the two troops of cavalry there go under my command and escort Carr and overtake the Fifth, if possible, to enable him to join his regiment. The troops consisting of Troops H and I, Tenth Cavalry, were officered by myself and Captain Graham, Lieutenants Banzhaf, Amick, and Orleman, and were soon in readiness for the duty required. We had returned from the relief of Forsyth Oct. 1st, and we started with Carr at 10:00 a.m. Oct. 14.

I concluded to march north so as to strike the Beaver as soon as possible, and then to follow down that creek with the expectation of finding the Fifth Cavalry or of striking its trail. On the fifteenth, I reached the Beaver at about 1:00 p.m., and after proceeding some miles down, went into bivouac. As we expected, we found a very large Indian trail about two weeks old, over which over two thousand head of ponies had been ridden or driven, going in the same direction.

The next day we continued our journey down the stream, finding plenty of water, a fine bottom covered with grass and timber, and still observing the Indian trail, which ran to a point about twenty miles east from the place where we first struck the Beaver. At this locality, the signs showed that the Indians had encamped for the night. The ground was covered for acres with old fireplaces, pieces of wood, and the manure of ponies; and a little distance off we found a dead Cheyenne, wrapped in his robes, lying upon a scaffolding in a tree, a protection against ravenous wolves. The trail then struck south toward Short Nose Creek, the Indian name for a stream about twenty miles south of the Beaver.

We continued our course, however, on the Beaver, until we made about thirty miles, and then stopped for the night.

As there was no pack outfit at Wallace, I was compelled to take wagons to carry our supplies, and had eleven with me. The mules, dragging heavy loads over rough country, were made to trot in order to keep up with the cavalry column. We had now moved down the Beaver about forty-five miles without finding anything about the Fifth, and it began to look as if something had taken the regiment in another direction.

The next morning, I sent Lieutenant Amick and ten men well mounted with Sharp Grover, the famous scout, with orders to proceed as quickly as possible across country to the Short Nose to look for signs of the Fifth Cavalry and to keep a sharp lookout for Indians.

Grover had been with Forsyth and afterward joined my command. He had married a Sioux woman and had lived for years with the Indians before the outbreak of hostilities. He could speak their language and knew their ways and customs, and was perfectly trained in reading signs. It was interesting to see how he could read what the tracks meant, as if they had been books. He could tell how long since the tracks were made, whether they were made by horses or ponies, shod or unshod, how many were ridden, how many were driven, whether it was a war party or a party changing camp. If Indians stopped for the night he could tell how many men or squaws were in the party, to what tribe they belonged, from the shape of their moccasins, and many more details. Like most of his ilk, Grover drank heavily on occasion. When the Indians went on the warpath, Grover could not stay longer with the Sioux, as his life was not safe, and he entered the government employ, where he rendered heroic and invaluable services. Later he was killed in a row at Pond City, near Fort Wallace.

Amick and his party soon disappeared over the hills to our right and we kept on down the stream, the general course of which was to the northeast. I began to feel certain that the Fifth Cavalry had never reached the Beaver, and that we would probably be attacked by the Indians if this was the case. Under these circumstances I felt that it would be wise to be cautious and on the lookout against surprise. The road we passed over was very rough and the stream in most places ran through deep-cut banks several feet high, with very few places suitable for crossing.

As night came on a place was selected for a camp in a bend of the creek where the wagons could be placed across, giving room inside to graze the animals without fear of a stampede from howling savages. Amick returned just before night, having scouted some miles beyond the Short Nose without discovering any trace of the Fifth Cavalry. Grover told me that as they passed across the divide between the Beaver and the Short Nose he came across a single Indian pony track. This track was coming from a direction to our rear, and showed that the pony was going at a rapid gallop.

Grover inferred from this that it was probably an Indian hunter returning homeward who had most likely crossed our trail behind us, discovered our presence in the country, and was riding as fast as possible to carry the news to the Indian camps somewhere to our front and not far off.

After a council over the situation, General Carr came to the conclusion, after having traveled some sixty miles down the Beaver without finding the Fifth, that the regiment had never reached that stream and that therefore he would give it up and start on our return in the morning.

About 7:00 a.m. on the next day, Oct. 15, Captain Graham expressed a wish to make a scout for a short distance to the front, and rode forward with two men. The command was ordered saddled up and everything made in readiness to move. In view of the fact that the south side of the creek was hilly and difficult and offered opportunities for ambuscades, I determined to go back by the north side, which was comparatively open. The afternoon before I had sent Lieutenant Orleman with a detachment to dig down the sides of the creek and prepare a practicable passage for the wagons and troops.

Graham had hardly ridden a thousand yards when twenty-five Indians suddenly dashed over the hill to his rear, with the evident intention of cutting him off. They were almost upon Graham before he discerned them, but he instantly struck spurs into his horse and dashed for the creek, the Indians firing a volley at short range upon the party. One of the bullets passed through Graham's hat, another through his coat, and a third through his leggings without wounding him. One of the horses was shot through the shoulder and fell. His rider succeeded in getting into the creek and behind the bank along with the other soldiers, and they commenced firing upon the Indians. Graham's girth burst as his horse sprang away at the first fire, but as his saddle gave way he seized his horse's mane and dragged himself forward on the animal. He then dashed the horse over the bank of the creek, about ten feet to the bottom. He fell from his horse in this jump, but the horse, fortunately, ran in our direction.

By this time, I started out thirty men under Lieutenants Amick and Orleman to cover the retreat of Graham's men. As they charged toward the hill the savages rushed from the creek to avoid being cut off, and were hotly pursued by our men. Judging that the presence of these Indians indicated that a large party could not be far off, I thought it best to be prudent and sent a trumpeter to overtake Amick and tell him to discontinue the pursuit and fall back slowly to camp. Without further delay I now broke up the camp, crossed the creek with wagons and troops, and, having dismounted the men, deployed them as riflemen to cover the retreat of Amick.

In a few minutes the absent party made its appearance on the hills, with bodies of Indians, numbering at least a hundred, skirmishing on our flank and rear. They slowly fell back toward the creek, and when within range the dismounted men on the banks opened fire on the advancing savages, and under cover of this Amick crossed and joined the command, while the Indians kept at a respectful distance.

The wagons were now placed in double column so as to make everything as compact as possible. H Troop was assigned on the flanks and advance, deployed in open order. Troop I covered the rear in the same manner, with one platoon under Graham as a reserve. These arrangements being completed, we moved steadily up the creek bottom. As soon as this movement commenced, a large body of Indians made their appearance and charged toward us, taking advantage of ravines, trees, and bluffs to fire from the south side of the creek. Some of the balls were well aimed and came close.

I soon saw that if we continued down the creek bottom the enemy would harass us immensely under cover of the timber and banks, and therefore changed our course so as to leave the valley and take the higher ground or divide. The Indians followed, showing about two hundred strong, and acted boldly in their attacks on the rear and flanks. The men and officers behaved very coolly, facing toward the enemy and driving them back without stopping the progress of the column.

At one point, we passed near a deep ravine, and the enemy, quick to observe cover of any kind, occupied it with quite a number of warriors and opened up a serious fire. The reserve platoon under Graham charged at the place as we were passing and, arriving at the edge of the ravine, poured in a volley at close range on the savages. A number must have been hurt and the Indians certainly lost no time in getting out of their position. Afterward they were more cautious in occupying ground too close to us. The flankers, under Banzhaf and Orleman, also repulsed the Indians on several occasions.

One Indian carried a red flag with some white device upon it, and by his movements the whole force seemed more or less governed. They were all stripped to the waists, and were decorated by various ornaments hanging from their heads and their shields, quivers, and bridles, so as to glisten and shine in the sun at every turn of the ponies. Up to this time five Indians were known to be killed at various points and quite a number wounded.

At 1:00 p.m., the enemy seemed to stop the fight and apparently withdrew, and I supposed that I had seen the last of them; but half an hour afterward, hearing an exclamation, I looked back and saw the Indians appearing again on the hills to our rear. On they came, one body after another coming in sight until it was estimated by all present that at least six hundred warriors were in view. Emboldened by their number they rushed forward, directing themselves toward our front, flanks and rear, making things look rather serious. I soon saw that we could not continue the march and meet this force, but that we must select a position and make a stand.

In the first attack in the morning I had offered the command to General Carr, as the senior officer present, but he declined it, stating that he considered himself simply as a passenger to be escorted, and I therefore continued to direct the operations.

I looked around and saw a small knoll or rise a short distance to the front, from which the ground fell in every direction, and this point was immediately selected. The teamsters were directed to take the trot, aim for this place, and on arrival at the knoll immediately to form a circular corral, half a circle on either side, with the mules facing inward, affording a shelter within and something of a fortification. As soon as we increased our pace, the Indians evidently thought we were running from them, and sent up a yell which made shivers run down the backs of some of our recruits. We kept on, however, at a fast gait, and the moment we struck the highest ground, the wagons were corralled with six wagons on one side, five wagons on the other, and the troops were rushed inside at a gallop and dismounted. The horses were tied together inside the corral with some men to watch them, and the rest were formed outside the corral in open order. This was done in about two minutes and then the advance of the Indians was upon us.

A fire commenced from our seven-shooter Spencers which sounded like the fire of a line of infantry. Indians charged up around the wagons, firing rapidly, and seriously wounded some of the men, but in a very short time they were driven back in wild disorder, leaving the ground covered with ponies, arms, and some bodies. Three dead warriors lay within fifty feet of the wagons. One man who was killed here was carried off by his comrades.

The chief Medicine Man, on a fine-looking horse, rode out in front of our line about two hundred yards off, after the retreat of the Indians, to try to show that his medicine was good and the white man's bullets could not hurt him. I directed several men near me to aim carefully at him. They fired and the Medicine Man went down, accompanied by a howl from the more distant Indians. After the repulse the men rushed forward from the wagons, seized and hauled in ten bodies of the Indians. The savages, disheartened and surprised at this reception, withdrew out of gunshot and assembled, apparently for council.

The men unloaded corn sacks and made breastworks near the wagons and we waited, expecting a renewal of the attack, for about an hour, when it became evident that some of the Indians were withdrawing. The day was very warm, we had been engaged about eight hours, and in the hot sun men and animals were suffering very much from thirst. I made up my mind to move for water, and keeping the wagons in double column, the horses inside and the men dismounted on the outside, we marched for the Beaver. A large party of Indians followed up to where their dead comrades lay and set up a mournful howl over their remains. Their loss in this fight, added to what they had suffered the month before in the conflict with Forsyth, must have had a sobering effect.

We now proceeded to the creek without further interference, and selecting a wide bottom encamped for the night, preparing some rifle pits to cover our outlying pickets and to enable them to receive the enemy if an attack were made in the morning. We heard them around us all night imitating coyotes, but they did not find a weak place and refrained from molesting us.

The next morning the Indians were gone and we marched by the shortest route to Fort Wallace, arriving there on the twenty-first.

On our return journey, we passed through Sheridan City, a frontier town located at the then terminus of the Kansas Division of the Union Pacific Railroad. It was full of taverns, saloons, gambling houses and dens, and of a rather tough lot of citizens and desperadoes. These people and others crowded into the streets when we passed through, and when they saw the troopers and their horses decorated with the spoils from the Indians whose dead bodies we had captured, they knew that we had been in a successful fight and they gave us a perfect ovation.

The savages suffered a considerable loss, but we escaped with a few men wounded (some of them seriously) and none killed. General Carr found the Fifth Cavalry had returned to the railroad, and through mistake they never reached the Beaver. He took command of the regiment, marched again and pursued the Indians over the Platte River, and followed them on a long campaign.

Sitting Bull's Account of the Battle at the Little Big Horn

The following is Sitting Bull's account as related to a reporter of a leading newspaper.

Through the intercession of a Major Walsh, Sitting Bull was persuaded at nightfall to hold a special conference with me. It was explained to him that I was not his enemy, but that I was his good friend. He was told by Major Walsh that I was a great paper chief; one who talked with a million tongues to all the people in the world. Said the Major: "This man is a man of wonderful medicine; he speaks, and the people on this side and across the great water open their ears and hear him. He tells the truth; he does not lie. He wishes to make the world know what a great tribe is encamped here on the land owned by the White Mother. [This interview took place at Fort Walsh, on British Territory, and the

"White Mother" here mentioned is Queen Victoria.] He wants it understood that her guests are mighty warriors. The Long-Haired Chief (alluding to General Custer) was his friend. He wants to hear from you how he fought and whether he met death like a brave."

"Agh-howgh!" (It is well) said Sitting Bull.

He finally agreed to come, after dark, to the quarters which had been assigned to me, on the condition that nobody should be present except myself, his interlocutor, Major Walsh, two interpreters, and the stenographer I had employed for the occasion.

At the appointed time, half-past eight, the lamps were lighted, and the most mysterious Indian Chieftain who ever flourished in North America was ushered in by Major Walsh, who locked the door behind him. This was the first time that Sitting Bull had condescended, not merely to visit but to address a white man from the United States. During the long years of his domination he had withstood, with his hands, every attempt on the part of the United States government at a compromise of interests. He had refused all proffers, declined any treaty. He had never been beaten in a battle with United States troops; on the contrary, his warriors had been victorious over the pride of our army. Pressed hard, he had retreated, scorning the factions of his bands who accepted the terms offered them, with the same bitterness with which he scorned his white enemies.

Here he stood, his blanket rolled back, his head upreared, his right moccasin put forward, his right hand thrown across his chest.

I arose and approached him, holding out both hands. He grasped them cordially.

"How!" said he.

"How!"

And now let me attempt a better portrait of Sitting Bull. He is about five feet, ten inches high. He was clad in a black and white calico shirt, black cloth leggings and moccasins, magnificently embroidered with beads and porcupine quills. He held in his left hand a fox-skin cap, its brush drooping to his feet; with the dignity and grace of a natural gentleman he had removed it from his head at the threshold. His long, black hair hung far down his back, athwart his cheeks and in front of his shoulders. His eyes gleamed like black diamonds. His visage, devoid of paint, was noble and commanding; nay, it was something more. Besides the Indian character given to it by high cheekbones, a broad, retreating forehead, a prominent, aquiline nose, and a jaw like a bull dog's, there was about the mouth something of beauty, but more of an expression of exquisite, cruel irony. Such a mouth and such eyes as this Indian's, if seen in the countenance of a white man, would appear to denote qualities similar to those which animated the career of Mazarin and inspired the pen of Machiavelli.

Yet there was something fearfully sweet in his smile as he extended to me his hands.

Such hands! They felt as small and soft as a maiden's, but when I pressed them I could feel the sinews beneath the flesh quivering hard, like a wild animal's. I led him to a seat, a lounge set against the wall, on which he sank with indolent grace. Major Walsh, brilliant in red uniform, sat beside him, and a portable table was brought near. Two interpreters brought chairs and seated themselves, and at a neighboring desk the stenographer took his place. I afterward learned that two Sioux chiefs stood on guard outside the door, and that all the Indians in the fort had their arms ready to spring in case of a suspected treachery. On the previous night, two of the Indians had been taken suddenly ill, and their sickness had been ascribed by some warriors to poison. So restless and anxious were all the savages that nothing but the influence and tact of Major Walsh could have procured for me and for your readers the following valuable, indeed, historical, colloquy with the Sphinx of the Northwest.

I turned to the interpreter and said:

"Explain again to Sitting Bull that he is with a friend."

The interpreter explained.

"Banee!" said the chief, holding out his hand again and pressing mine.

Major Walsh here said: "Sitting Bull is in the best mood now that you could possibly wish. Proceed with your questions, and make them as logical as you can. I will assist you, and trip you up occasionally if you are likely to irritate him."

Then the dialogue went on. I give it literally.

"You are a great chief," said I to Sitting Bull, "but you live behind a cloud. Your face is dark; my people do not see it. Tell me, do you hate the Americans very much?"

A gleam as of fire shot across his face.

"I am no chief."

This was precisely what I expected. It will dissipate at once the erroneous idea which has prevailed, that Sitting Bull is either a chief or a warrior.

"What are you?"

"I am," said he, crossing both hands upon his chest, slightly nodding, and smiling satirically, "a man."

"What does he mean?" I inquired, turning to Major Walsh.

"He means," responded the Major, "to keep you in ignorance of his secret if he can. His position among his bands is anomalous. His own tribes, the Uncpapas, are not all in fealty to him. Parts of nearly twenty different tribes of Sioux, besides a remnant of the Uncpapas, abide with him. So far as I have learned, he rules over these fragments of tribes, which compose his camp of twenty-five hundred, including between eight hundred and nine hundred warriors, by sheer compelling force of intellect and will. I believe that he understands nothing particularly of war or military tactics, at least not enough to give him the skill or the right to command warriors in battle. He is supposed to have guided the fortunes of several battles, including the fight in which Custer fell. That supposition, as you will presently find, is partially erroneous. His word was always potent in the camp or in the field, but he has usually left to the war chiefs the duties appertaining to engagements. When the crisis came, he gave his opinion, which was accepted as law."

"What was he then?" I inquired, continuing this momentary dialogue with Major Walsh. "Was he, is he, a mere medicine man?"

"Don't for the world," replied the Major, "intimate to him, in the questions you are about to ask him, that you have derived the idea from me, or from any one, that he is a mere medicine man. He would deem that to be a profound insult. In point of fact he is a medicine man, but a far greater, more influential medicine man than any savage I have ever known. He has constituted himself a ruler. He is a unique power among the Indians. His power consists in the universal confidence which is given to his judgment, which he seldom denotes until he is asked for an expression of it. It has been, so far, so accurate, it has guided his people so well, he has been caught in so few mistakes and he has saved even his ablest and oldest chiefs from so many evil consequences of their own misjudgment, that today his word among them all, is worth more than the united voices of the rest of the camp. He speaks. They listen and they obey. Now let us hear what his explanation will be."

"You say you are no chief?"

"No!" with considerable hauteur.

"Are you a head soldier?"

"I am nothing—neither a chief nor a soldier."

"What? Nothing?"

"Nothing."

"What, then, makes the warriors of your camp, the great chiefs who are here along with you, look up to you so? Why do they think so much of you?"

Sitting Bull's lips curled with a proud smile.

"Oh, I used to be a kind of a chief; but the Americans made me go away from my father's hunting ground."

"You do not love the Americans?"

You should have seen this savage's lips.

"I saw today that all the warriors around you clapped their hands and cried out when you spoke. What you said appeared to please them. They liked you. They seemed to think that what you said was right for them to say. If you are not a great chief, why do these men think so much of you?"

At this Sitting Bull, who had in the meantime been leaning back against the wall, assumed a posture of mingled toleration and disdain.

"Your people look up to men because they are rich; because they have much land, many lodges, many squaws?"

"Yes."

"Well, I suppose my people look up to me because I am poor. That is the difference."

In this answer was concentrated all the evasiveness natural to an Indian.

"What is your feeling toward the Americans now?"

He did not even deign an answer. He touched his hip, where his knife was.

I asked the interpreter to insist on an answer.

"Listen," said Sitting Bull, not changing his posture, but putting his right hand out upon my knee. "I told them today what my notions were—that I did not want to go back there. Every time that I had any difficulty with them they struck me first. I want to live in peace."

"Have you an implacable enmity to the Americans? Would you live with them in peace if they allowed you to do so; or do you think that you can only obtain peace here?"

"The White Mother is good."

"Better than the Great Father?"

"Howgh!"

And then after a pause, Sitting Bull continued. "They asked me to-day to give them my horses. I bought my horses, and they are mine. I bought them from men who came up the Missouri in mackinaws. They do not belong to the Government, neither do the rifles. The rifles are also mine. I bought them; I paid for them. Why I should give them up I do not know. I will not give them up."

"Do you really think, do your people believe, that it is wise to reject the proffers that have been made to you by the United States Commissioners? Do not some of you feel as if you were destined to lose your old hunting grounds? Don't you see that you will probably have the same difficulty in Canada that you have had in the United States?"

"The White Mother does not lie."

"Do you expect to live here by hunting? Are there buffaloes enough? Can your people subsist on the game here?"

"I don't know; I hope so."

"If not, are any part of your people disposed to take up agriculture? Would any of them raise steers and go to farming?"

"I don't know."

"What will they do, then?"

"As long as there are buffaloes, that is the way we will live."

"But the time will come when there will be no more buffaloes."

"Those are the words of an American."

"How long do you think the buffaloes will last?"

Sitting Bull arose. "We know," said he, extending his right hand with an impressive gesture, "that on the other side the buffaloes will not last very long. Why? Because the country there is poisoned with blood—a poison that kills all the buffaloes drives them away. It is strange," he continued, with his peculiar smile, "that the Americans should complain that the Indians kill buffaloes. We kill buffaloes, as we kill other animals, for food and clothing, to make our lodges warm. They kill buffaloes—for what? Go through your country. See the thousands of carcasses rotting on the Plains. Your young men shoot for pleasure. All they take from a dead buffalo is his tail, or his head, or his horns, perhaps, to show they have killed a buffalo. What is this? Is it robbery? You call us savages. What are they? The buffaloes have come

North. We have come North to find them, and to get away from a place where the people tell lies."

To gain time, and not to dwell importunately on a single point, I asked Sitting Bull to tell me something of his early life. In the first place, where he was born?

"I was born on the Missouri River; at least I recollect that some-body told me so—I don't know who told me or where I was told of it."

"Of what tribe are you?"

"I am an Uncpapa."

"Of the Sioux?"

"Yes; of the great Sioux Nation."

"Who was your father?"

"My father is dead."

"Is your mother living?"

"My mother lives with me in my lodge."

"Great lies are told about you. White men say that you lived among them when you were young; that you went to school; that you learned to write and read from books; that you speak English; that you know how to talk French?"

"It is a lie."

"You are an Indian?"

(Proudly) "I am a Sioux."

Then, suddenly relaxing from his hauteur, Sitting Bull began to laugh. "I have heard," he said, "of some of these stories. They are all strange lies. What I am I am," and here he leaned back and resumed his attitude and expression of barbaric grandeur.

"I am a man. I see. I know. I began to see when I was not yet born; when I was not in my mother's arms. It was then I began to study about my people. I studied about many things. I studied about the smallpox, that was killing my people—the great sickness that was killing the women and children. I was so interested that I turned over on my side. The God Almighty must have told me at that time [and here Sitting

Bull unconsciously revealed his secret], that I would be the man to be the judge of all the other Indians—a big man, to decide for them in all their ways."

"And you have since decided for them?"

"I speak. It is enough."

"Could not your people, whom you love so well, get on with Americans?"

"No!"

"Why?"

"I never taught my people to trust Americans. I have told them the truth—that the Americans are great liars. I have never dealt with the Americans. Why should I? The land belonged to my people. I say I never dealt with them—I mean I never treated them in a way to surrender my people's rights. I treated with them, but I always gave full value for what I got. I never asked the United States Government to make me presents of blankets or cloth, or anything of that kind. The most I did was to ask them to send me an honest trader that I could trade with, and I proposed to give him buffalo robes and elk skins, and other hides in exchange for what we wanted. I told every trader who came to our camps that I did not want any favors from him—that I wanted to trade with him fairly and equally, giving him full value for what I got, but the traders wanted me to trade with them on no such terms. They wanted to give little and get much. They told me if I did not accept what they give me in trade they would get the government to fight me. I told them I did not want to fight."

"But you fought?"

"At last, yes; but not until I had tried hard to prevent a fight. At first my young men, when they began to talk bad, stole five American horses. I took the horses away from them and gave them back to the Americans. It did no good. By and by we had to fight."

It was at this juncture that I began to question the great savage before me in regard to the most disastrous, most mysterious Indian battle of the century—Custer's encounter with the Sioux on the Big Horn—the Thermopylæ of the plains. Sitting Bull, the chief genius of his bands, has been supposed to have commanded the Sioux forces when Custer fell.

That the reader may understand Sitting Bull's statements, it will be necessary for him to read the following preliminary sketch. It should be understood, moreover, that, inasmuch as every white man with Custer perished, and no other white man, save one or two scouts, had conferred carefully with Sitting Bull or any of his chiefs since that awful day, this is the first authentic story of the conflict which can possibly have appeared out of the lips of a survivor. It has the more historical value, since it comes from the chief among Custer's and Reno's foes.

Custer, on June 22, started up the Rosebud, with the following order from General Terry in his pocket—

"Lieutenant-Colonel Custer, Seventh Cavalry.

"COLONEL: The brigadier-general commanding directs that as soon as your regiment can be made ready for the march, you proceed up the Rosebud in pursuit of the Indians whose trail was discovered by Major Reno a few days since. It is, of course, impossible to give definite instructions in regard to this movement, and, were it not impossible to do so, the department commander places too much confidence in your zeal, energy, and ability, to wish to impose upon you precise orders which might hamper your action when nearly in contact with the enemy. He will, however, indicate to you his own views of what your action should be, and he desires that you should conform to them unless you shall see sufficient reason for departing from them. He thinks that you should proceed up the Rosebud until you ascertain definitely the direction in which the trail above spoken of leads. Should it be found, as it appears to be almost certain that it will be to turn toward the Little Big Horn, he thinks that you should still proceed southward, perhaps as far as the headwaters of the Tongue, and then turn toward the Little Big Horn, feeling constantly, however, toward your left, so as to preclude the possibility of the escape of the Indians to the south or southeast by passing around your left flank. The column of Colonel Gibbon is now in motion for the mouth of the Big Horn. As soon as it reaches that point it will cross the Yellowstone and move up at least as far as the parks of the Big and Little Big Horn. Of course, its future movements must be controlled by circumstances as they arise; but it is hoped that the Indians, if upon the Little Big Horn, may be so nearly enclosed by two columns that their escape will be impossible. The department commander desires that on your way up the Rosebud you should thoroughly examine the upper part of Tulloch's Creek, and that you should endeavor to send a scout through to Colonel Gibbon's column with information of the result of your examination. The lower part of this creek will be examined by a detachment of Colonel Gibbon's command. The supply steamer will be pushed up the Big Horn as far as the forks of the river are found to be navigable for that space, and the department commander, who will accompany the column of Colonel Gibbon, desires you to report to him there not later than the expiration of the time for which your troops are rationed, unless in the meantime you receive further orders.

Respectfully,

E. W. SMITH,

Captain Eighteenth Infantry, Acting Assistant Adjutant-General."

With these tentative instructions, General Custer proceeded on his way. Hearing of the Indians, he found that he had a great opportunity to strike them. He touched their trail and followed it. He laid his plans, with what lack of success we know. But shall we not also inquire what was the real cause of his untimely, unnecessary failure?

General Custer had been chided for a division of his troops. In point of fact he never attacked an Indian camp when he had more than a company, without so separating his command as to encompass, bewilder, and capture it. We shall presently see whether it was the fault of his dispositions on this occasion which lost him his last battle. Here is Reno's account of the way in which the commands respectively, under Custer, himself, and Benteen, started into action:

"The regiment left the camp at the mouth of Rosebud River, after passing in review before the department commander, under command of Brevet Major General G. A. Custer, Lieutenant-Colonel, on the afternoon of June 22, and marched up the Rosebud twelve miles and encamped. On the 23rd, marched up the Rosebud, passing many old Indian camps, and following a very large lodge-pole trail, but not fresh, making thirty-three miles. On the 24th, the march was continued up the Rosebud, the trail and signs freshening with every mile, until we had made twenty-eight miles, and we then encamped and waited for information from the scouts. At 9:25 p.m. Custer called the officers together and informed us that, beyond a doubt, the village was in the valley of the Little Big Horn, and that to reach it, it was necessary to cross the divide between the Rosebud and Little Big Horn, and that it would be impossible to do so in the daytime without discovering our march to the Indians; that we would prepare to move at 11:00 p.m. This was done, the line of march turning from the Rosebud to the right, up one of its branches, which headed near the summit at the divide.

"About 2:00 p.m. on the twenty-fifth, the scouts told him that he could not cross the divide before daylight. We then made coffee and rested three hours, at the expiration of which time the march was resumed, the divide crossed, and about 8:00 a.m., the command was in the valley of one of the branches of the Little Big Horn. By this time the Indians had been seen, and it was certain that we could not surprise them, and it was determined to move at once to the attack.

"Previous to this no division of the regiment had been made since the order was issued on the Yellowstone annulling wing and battalion organizations. General Custer informed me he would assign commands on the march. I was ordered by Lieut. W. W. Cook, adjutant, to assume command of Companies M, A, and G, Capt. Benteen of Companies H, D, and K, Custer retaining C, E, F, I, and L under his immediate command, and Company B, Capt. McDougall, in rear of the pack train. I assumed command of the companies assigned to me, and without any definite orders moved forward the rest of the column and well to its left. I saw Benteen moving further to the left, and as they passed he told me he had orders to move well to the left and sweep everything before him. I did not see him again until about 2:30 p.m. The command moved down the creek toward the Little Big Horn Valley, Custer, and five companies, on the right bank, myself and three companies on the left bank, and Benteen further to the left and out of sight."

It appears to have been about the middle of the forenoon when Custer thus subdivided his column. Reno goes on to say that at half past twelve Lieut. Cook, Custer's adjutant, came to him, told him that the village was only two miles away, and ordered him to move forward rapidly and charge it. Other evidence likewise shows that this order was given about that time, and that Reno was urged not to let up on the Indians. The Indian village, consisting of camps of Cheyennes, Ogallalas, Minneconjous, and Uncpapas, was nearly three miles long. Reno crossed the Little Big Horn, formed his first line just south of the crossing and charged. He says:

"I deployed, and, with the Ree scouts at my left, charged down the valley with great ease for about two and a half miles."

Reno, instead of holding the ground thus gained, retreated, being hard pressed. He made a temporary stand in a bunch of timber, but finally retreated back over the valley, and across the Little Big Horn and up the bluffs, on the summit of which he intrenched himself late in the afternoon.

Custer's march to the ford, where he attempted to cross the Little Big Horn and attack the Indians in their rear, was much longer than Reno's march, consequently Custer's assault was not made until after Reno's. Custer's intention was to sandwich, as it were, the main body of the Indians between Reno's and his own forces. He hoped by thus pressing them on two sides—Reno constantly fighting them and he himself constantly fighting them—to disconcert them and crush them at last. His plan is thus seen to have been that of a general. It relieves him from the aspersion of rashness. It must, in this connection, be remembered that Custer had fought Indians many times and had never been beaten by them, although on several occasions he had encountered more than three times the number of his own troops. He trusted in this instance to the fealty of his own officers, the bravery of his soldiers, and his own genius to overcome the mere weight of numbers, as he had so often done before.

The testimony of Sitting Bull which I am about to give, is the more convincing and important from the very fact of the one erroneous impression he derived as to the identity of the officer in command of the forces which assailed his camp. He confounds Reno with Custer. He supposes that one and the same general crossed the Little Big Horn where Reno crossed, charged as Reno charged, retreated as Reno retreated back over the river, and then pursued the line of Custer's march, attacked as Custer attacked, and fell as Custer fell.

"Did you know the Long Haired Chief?" I asked Sitting Bull.

"No."

"What! Had you never seen him?"

"No. Many of the chiefs knew him."

"What do they think of him?"

"He was a great warrior."

"Was he brave?"

"He was a mighty chief."

"Now, tell me. Here is something I wish to know. Big lies are told about the fight in which the Long-Haired Chief was killed. He was my friend. No one has come back to tell the truth about him, or about that fight. You were there; you know. Your chiefs know. I want to hear something that forked tongues do not tell—the truth."

"It is well."

Here I drew forth a map of the battlefield and spread it out across Sitting Bull's knees and explained to him the names and situations as represented on it, and he smiled.

"We thought we were whipped," he said.

"Ah! Did you think the soldiers were too many for you?"

"Not at first; but by-and-by, yes. Afterwards, no."

"Tell me about the battle. Where was the Indian camp first attacked?"

"Here" (pointing to Reno's crossing on the map).

"About what time in the day was that?"

"It was some two hours past the time when the sun is in the center of the sky."

"What white chief was it who came over there against your warriors?"

"The Long Hair."

"Are you sure?"

"The Long Hair commanded."

"But you did not see him?"

"I have said that I never saw him."

"Did any of the chiefs see him?"

"Not here, but there," pointing to the place where Custer charged and was repulsed, on the north bank to the Little Big Horn.

"Why do you think it was the Long Hair who crossed first and charged you here at the right side of the map?"

"A chief leads his warriors."

"Was there a good fight here, on the right side of the map? Explain it to me?"

"It was so," said Sitting Bull, raising his hands. "I was lying in my lodge. Some young men ran in to me and said: 'The Long Hair is in the camp. Get up. They are firing in the camp.' I said, all right, and jumped up and stepped out of my lodge."

"Where was your lodge?"

"Here, with my people," answered Sitting Bull, pointing to the group of Uncpapa lodges, designated as "abandoned lodges" on the map.

"So the first attack was made, then, on the right side of the map, and upon the lodges of the Uncpapas?"

"Yes."

"Here the lodges are said to have been deserted?"

"The old men, the squaws, and the children were hurried away."

"Toward the other end of the camp?"

"Yes. Some of the Minneconjou women and children also left their lodges when the attack began."

"Did you retreat at first?"

"Do you mean the warriors?"

"Yes, the fighting men."

"Oh, we fell back, but it was not what warriors call a retreat; it was to gain time. It was the Long Hair who retreated. My people fought him here in the brush [designating the timber behind which the Indians pressed Reno] and he fell back across [placing his finger on the line of Reno's retreat to the northern bluffs]."

"So you think that was the Long Hair whom your people fought in that timber and who fell back afterwards to those heights?"

"Of course."

"What occurred afterward? Was there any heavy fighting after the retreat of the soldiers to the bluffs?"

"Not then; not there."

"Where, then?"

"Why, down here," and Sitting Bull indicated with his finger the place where Custer approached and touched the river. "That," said he, "was where the big fight was fought a little later. After the Long Hair was driven back to the bluffs he took this road [tracing with his finger the line of Custer's march on the map], and went down to see if he could not beat us there."

(Here the reader should pause to discern the extent of Sitting Bull's error, and to anticipate what will presently appear to be Reno's misconception or mistake. Sitting Bull, not identifying Reno in the whole of this engagement, makes it seem that it was Custer who attacked, when Reno attacked in the first place, and afterward moved down to resume the assault from a new position. He thus involuntarily testifies to the fact that Reno's assault was a brief, ineffectual one before his retreat to the bluffs, and that Reno, after his retreat, ceased on the bluffs from aggressive fighting.)

"When the fight commenced here," I asked, pointing to the spot where Custer advanced behind the Little Big Horn, "what happened?"

"Hell!"

"You mean, I suppose, a fierce battle?"

"I mean a thousand devils."

"The village was by this time thoroughly aroused?"

"The squaws were like flying birds; the bullets were like humming bees."

"You say that when the first attack was made off here on the right of the map, the old men and squaws and children ran down the valley toward the left. What did they do when this second attack came from up here toward the left?"

"They ran back again to the right, here and there," answered Sitting Bull, placing his swarthy fingers on the words "Abandoned Lodges."

"And where did the warriors run?"

"They ran to the fight—the big fight."

"So that in the afternoon, after the first fight, on the right-hand side of the map, was over, and after the big fight on the left-hand side began, you say the squaws and children all returned to the right hand side, and that the warriors, the fighting men of all the Indian camps, ran to the place where the big fight was going on?"

"Yes."

"Why was that? Were not some of the warriors left in front of these intrenchments on the bluffs, near the right side of the map? Did not you think it necessary—did not your war chiefs think it necessary—to keep some of your young men there to fight the troops who had retreated to these intrenchments?"

"No."

"Why?"

"You have forgotten."

"How?"

"You forget that only a few soldiers were left by the Long Hair on those bluffs. He took the main body of his soldiers with him to make the big fight down here on the left."

"So there were no soldiers to make a fight left in the intrenchments on the right-hand bluff?"

"I have spoken. It is enough. The squaws could deal with them. There were none but squaws and pappooses in front of them that afternoon."

This startling assertion of Sitting Bull involves the most terrible charge which has been brought against Reno. It amounts to an assertion, that Reno, having made his assault, been beaten and retreated, stayed there on the bluffs without renewing the attack for which Gen. Custer, who had by this time come down with his horsemen on the rear of the Sioux camp from the north, vainly awaited—how hopelessly!

"Well, then," I inquired of Sitting Bull, "did the cavalry, who came down and made the big fight, fight?"

Again, Sitting Bull smiled.

"They fought. Many young men are missing from our lodges. But is there an American squaw who has her husband left? Were there any Americans left to tell the story of that day?"

"No."

"How did they come on to the attack?"

"I have heard that there are trees which tremble."

"Do you mean the trees with trembling leaves?"

"Yes."

"They call them, in some parts of the Western country, Quaking Asps; in the eastern part of the country they call them Silver Aspens."

"Hah? A great white chief, whom I met once, spoke these words, 'Silver Aspens,' trees that shake; these were the Long Hair's soldiers."

"You do not mean that they trembled before your people because they were afraid?"

"They were brave men. They were tired. They were too tired."

"How did they act? How did they behave themselves?"

At this Sitting Bull again arose. I also arose from my seat, as did the other persons in the room, except the stenographer.

"Your people," said Sitting Bull, extending his right hand, "were killed. I tell no lies about dead men. These men who came with the Long Hair were as good men as ever fought. When they rode up their horses were tired and they were tired. When they got off from their horses they could not stand firmly on their feet. They swayed to and fro—so my young men have told me—like the limbs of cypresses in a great wind. Some of them staggered under the weight of their guns. But they began to fight at once; but by this time, as I have said, our camps were aroused, and there were plenty of warriors to meet them. They fired with needle guns. We replied with magazine guns—repeating rifles. It was so (and here Sitting Bull illustrated by patting his palms together with the rapidity of a fusillade). Our young men rained lead across the river and drove the white braves back."

"And then?"

"And then they rushed across themselves."

"And then?"

"And then they found that they had a good deal to do."

"Was there at that time some doubt about the issue of the battle, whether you would whip the Long Hair or not?"

"There was so much doubt about it that I started down there (here again, pointing to the map) to tell the squaws to pack up the lodges and get ready to move away."

"You were on that expedition, then, after the big fight had fairly begun?"

"Yes."

"You did not personally witness the rest of the big fight? You were not engaged in it?"

"No; I have heard of it from the warriors."

"When the great crowds of your young men crossed the river in front of the Long Hair, what did they do? Did they attempt to assault him directly in his front?"

"At first they did, but afterward they found it better to try and get around him. They formed themselves on all sides of him, except just at his back."

"How long did it take them to put themselves around his flanks?"

"As long as it takes the sun to travel from here to here" (indicating some marks upon his arm, with which, apparently, he is used to gauge the progress of the shadow of his lodge across his arm, and probably meaning half an hour. An Indian has no more definite way than this to express the lapse of time).

"The trouble was with the soldiers," he continued; "they were so exhausted, and their horses bothered them so much, that they could not take good aim. Some of their horses broke away from them and left them to stand and drop and die. When the Long Hair, the General, found that he was so outnumbered and threatened on his flanks, he took the best course he could have taken. The bugle blew. It was an order to fall back. All the men fell back fighting and dropping. They could not fire fast enough, though. But from our side it was so," said Sitting Bull, and here he clapped his hands rapidly, twice a second, to express with what quickness and continuance the balls flew from the Henry and Winchester rifles wielded by the Indians. "They could not stand up under such a fire," he added.

"Were any military tactics shown? Did the Long-Haired Chief make any disposition of his soldiers, or did it seem as though they retreated altogether, helter-skelter, fighting for their lives?"

"They kept in pretty good order. Some great chief must have commanded them all the while. They would fall back across a *coulie*, and make a fresh stand beyond, on higher ground. The map is pretty nearly right. It shows where the white men stopped and fought before they were all killed. I think that is right—down there to the left, just above the Little Big Horn. There was one party driven out there, away from the rest, and there a great many men were killed. The places marked on the map are pretty nearly the places where all were killed."

"Did the whole command keep on fighting until the last?"

"Every man, so far as my people could see. There were no cowards on either side."

Cowards! One would think not. The best testimony, from one who has examined the battlefield and the line of Custer's retreat, is as follows:

"From this point [the north bank of the Little Big Horn, where Custer was forced back by overpowering numbers] he was driven back to make successive stands on the higher ground. His line of retreat stretches from the river to the spot indicated on the map as that where he fell. On the line of retreat, Calhoun's company seems to have been thrown across it to check the Indians. At a distance of about three-quarters of a mile from the river, the whole of Calhoun's company lay dead in an irregular line, Calhoun and Crittenden in place in the rear. About a mile beyond this, on the ridge parallel to the stream, still following the line of retreat indicated on the map, Keogh's company was slaughtered in position, his right resting on the hill where Custer fell, and which seems to have been held by Yates's company. On the most prominent part of the ridge Custer made his last desperate stand. Here, with Captain Yates, Colonel Cook, Captain Custer, Lieutenant Riley, and others, and thirty-two men of Yates's command, he went down, fighting heroically to the last, against the tremendous odds which assailed them on all sides. It is believed by some that, finding the situation a desperate one, they killed their horses for a barricade. From the point where Custer fell, the line of retreat again doubles back toward the river through a ravine, and along this line in the ravine twenty-three bodies of Smith's company were found. Where this terminates, near the river, are found the dead men and horses of Captain Custer's company, commingled with Smith's, and the situation of the dead indicates that some desperate attempt was made to make a stand near the river, or to gain the woods."

I inquired of Sitting Bull: "How long did this big fight continue?"

"The sun was there," he answered, pointing to within two hours from the western horizon.

I went on to interrogate Sitting Bull:

"This big fight, then, extended through three hours?"

"Through most of the going forward of the sun."

"Where was the Long Hair most of the time?"

"I have talked with my people; I cannot find one who saw the Long Hair until just before he died. He did not wear his hair long as he used to wear it. His hair was like yours," said Sitting Bull, playfully touching my forehead with his fingers. "It was short, but it was of the color of the grass when the frost comes."

"Did you hear from your people how he died? Did he die on horseback?"

"No; none of them died on horseback."

"All were dismounted?"

"Yes."

"And Custer, the Long Hair?"

"Well, I have understood that there were a great many brave men in that fight, and that from time to time, while it was going on, they were shot down like pigs. They could not help themselves. One by one the officers fell. I believe the Long Hair rode across once from this place down here (meaning the place where Tom Custer's and Smith's companies were killed), to this place up here (indicating the spot on the map where Custer fell), but I am not sure about this. Anyway it was said that up there where the last fight took place, where the last stand was made, the Long Hair stood like a sheaf of corn with all the ears fallen around him."

"Not wounded?"

"No."

"How many stood by him?"

"A few."

"When did he fall?"

"He killed a man when he fell. He laughed."

"You mean he cried out?"

"No, he laughed; he had fired his last shot."

"From a carbine?"

"No, a pistol."

"Did he stand up after he first fell?"

"He rose up on his hands and tried another shot, but his pistol would not go off."

"Was anyone else standing up when he fell down?"

"One man was kneeling, that was all. But he died before the Long Hair. All this was far up on the bluffs, far away from the Sioux encampment. I did not see it. It was told to me. But it is true."

"The Long Hair was not scalped?"

"No; my people did not want his scalp."

"Why?"

"I have said he was a great chief."

"Did you at any time," I persisted, "during the progress of the fight, believe that your people would get the worst of it?"

"At one time, as I have told you, I started down to tell squaws to strike the lodges. I was then on my way up to the right end of the camp, where the first attack was made upon us. But before I reached that end of the camp, where the Minneconjou and Uncpapa squaws and children were, and where some of the other squaws—Cheyennes and Ogallalas—had gone, I was overtaken by one of the young warriors, who had just come from the fight. He called out to me. He said: 'No use to leave camp; every white man is killed.' So I stopped and went no further. I turned back, and by-and-by I met the warriors returning."

"But in the meantime," I asked, "were there no warriors occupied up here at the right end of the camp? Was nobody left, except the squaws and the children and the old men, to take care of that end of the camp? Was nobody ready to defend it against the soldiers in those intrenchments up there?"

"Oh," replied Sitting Bull again, "there was no need to waste warriors in that direction. There were only a few soldiers in those intrenchments, and we knew they wouldn't dare to come out."

This finished the interview, and with a few more How! Hows, the wily chieftain withdrew.

A Chase

Adapted from Fighting Indians in the Seventh United States Cavalry: Custer's Favorite Regiment *by Ami Frank Mulford*

We passed over the battlefield of 1874, where General Stanley and his command were so badly cut up by Sioux Indians. Bones were strewn on the ground quite thick. Here is the skeleton of a horse and close to it the skeleton of a man, the bare and bleached bones glistening in the sunlight, and the whitened skull looking grinningly up at us as we ride past. Near these bones we notice a dozen or more empty cartridge shells, sure proof that the soldier had died in the line of duty.

"Will our bones ever lie and bleach in such a place?" we wonder as we go on—to we know not what!

We now ride over a beautiful table land, flat and smooth as a barn floor. It forms a point made by the Yellowstone River and High Creek, where they join; then through badlands, cut up by deep ravines and gulches. Not a spear of grass or a bit of cactus or other growth relieves the eye. This is a land of desolation. We enter a deep ravine, and along the bottom we go, rock walls rise thirty, sixty, in places a hundred feet above our heads on either side. What a place for an ambuscade! But our scouts are ahead and it is safe to follow them.

Cutting sand and fine dust strike our faces, fill our eyes and make breathing difficult. Look, there are massive rocks ahead that block our way; no, we take a sharp turn to the right, and emerge from desolation directly into paradise! The finest, smoothest, largest meadow I ever saw is right before me—a meadow where a scythe has never been swung. The rich grass brushes the legs of the cavalrymen as they ride through it.

Halt—sounds the trumpet.

Dismount—it sounds again, and we get off our horses, remove the bits from their mouths and let them eat and be happy while they can. We are to wait here until the wagon train catches up with us.

General Miles is half a mile ahead of us with his scouts. He is signaling. What does that mean?

Indians!

The trumpet sounds *To Horse!*—and we quickly put the bits in our horses' mouths, and are ready.

Mount!—goes the trumpet, and we mount. There is no confusion, no misunderstanding the tones of the trumpet, for it is in the hands of Chief Trumpeter Hardy himself.

Forward—sounds the trumpet again, and forward we go. We make for that bluff where we can see General Miles.

When we had gone a quarter of a mile, we saw someone leave the bluff and ride full speed to intercept Trumpeter Hardy. The two meet. Trumpeter Hardy bends over in the saddle to receive an order, sent by General Miles, and then as he straightens up there is a bright flash in the sunlight. He has in hand the copper bugle he carried when he was with Custer during the Civil War. See! He raises it to his lips and the tones of the bugle sound out clear and strong. What melody! But what is the order?

Companies Right Into Line!—and putting ourselves into that position in an instant, we ride forward.

Gallop—is the next call. At last! Aha, this is something like it! Just what we had heard about but had given up all hopes of taking part in.

A Trumpeter of each company is with his Captain, and another stays by the First Sergeant of the Company. It is the duty of these company trumpeters to tell what the calls mean and to repeat them.

How our travel-worn horses do pull out, each doing its best.

Deploy Skirmishers, By the Right and Left Flank!—is the next call sounded, and the six companies of the Seventh Cavalry take their positions twenty yards apart, with horses on a gallop.

CHARGE!—commands the bugle of Chief Trumpeter Hardy. Twelve Company Trumpeters repeat this call, and on we go as fast as we can make our horses travel. We make the top of the bluff, and, whew! about two miles distant are about two score mounted Indian braves, and there may be several thousand more behind that other bluff. On we rush—but will the reds stand? No, they are off! See them lash their ponies. I hear them yell! Uphill and down we keep up the chase, but get no nearer the fugitives. Our horses are flecked with foam and many of them begin to lag. The wagon train and pack mules are out of sight.

We reach the top of a ridge, and on the flat land below, quietly resting on the bank of Cherry Creek, are our savages—those two score

Indians we have been trying so hard to catch. We have been chasing our own scouts, friendly Cheyennes and Crows, who had that morning been sent on ahead to scout for hostiles.

Recall was sounded, and *Rally by Companies* follows. We are soon in proper trim. Word was then passed along that General Miles, wishing to see how the Seventh Cavalry would respond in an emergency, had instructed the scouts to make the fake run, and they most successfully complied with his orders.

We went into camp. The wagon train and pack mules came in late.

General Miles Forces Chief Joseph to Yield— A Graphic Account

Adapted from Fighting Indians in the Seventh United States Cavalry: Custer's Favorite Regiment *by Ami Frank Mulford*

The general interest in the battle between Nez Perce warriors led by Chief Joseph, and the Cavalry force with General Miles in command, and the surrender of the hostiles, demands more attention than ever has appeared in print. It was the finale of an important campaign; it threw wide open the door that had blocked the way for the settlement of the Great Northwest; it stopped trespassing on the soil of a friendly nation by disgruntled natives of this country—our wards, not wanted there, whose best interests demanded that they should cease savagery and live in peace with their white neighbors.

When Chief Joseph started forth on this final and fateful campaign, he was in command of a large force of superior and well equipped Indian warriors. With these hostiles, it was a most sacred war. From the time they left their homes in Oregon, until they were attacked by the command of General Miles on Snake Creek, they had traveled sixteen hundred miles and at a rate that would have killed a cavalry horse.

This was a wonderful trip. Chief Joseph did not make it with warriors alone. He had with him all the squaws, children and aged males of the tribe, their tepees and other belongings. Joseph's movements were retarded, and at times diverted, by strong bodies of United States troops. He was able and shrewd, and was keen in leading pursuing columns along trails where their men and horses would suffer most for want of food and water.

Chief Joseph's warriors had dwindled to about three hundred; every one of them hardened by the difficulties of the march, able to go days without food or water, and each brave carrying a gun made for use in hunting large game. They also had a number of long range needle-guns, two of them being supplied with the most approved telescope sights. One of the rifles was a heavy Creedmore, such as is used by the most skillful shots in America on the celebrated ranges. No doubt it was one of these rifles that sent that bullet in the direction of General Sturges, during the brief skirmish at the Gap in the Mountains, which caused him to lower his field glass and step out of range.

The failure of General Howard to land Chief Joseph, is said to be due to the fact that Howard started on the chase with his command not half supplied with equipment necessary for such a drive. As a result, Howard's movements were hampered and his fighting strength greatly reduced at the time when his force should have been at its very best.

General Howard was not versed in Indian warfare. He found there is a vast difference between Agency life and its treaty-making, and fighting Indians. It was Howard's lack of tact that impelled Joseph and his brother White Bird and the rest of the Nez Perces to reject the demand of Howard. They did not want to fight; they wanted to escape to a land of refuge, where they could live in peace. This is the Indians' side of the story.

Chief Joseph continued on his retreat through the northern mountains. On August 9, General Gibbons came into ineffectual contact with him at the Big Hole Mountains.

When General Miles started from the mouth of Tongue River, September 18, to attack Chief Joseph, he had formed his plans so well that victory was assured. He struck Chief Joseph's camp September 30, 1877, after marching twelve days, at the very place he said he would before setting out from Tongue River. The men under Miles were eager for the fray. As soon as the Indians were seen General Miles, without hesitation, placed himself in front of the troops, and at once the first order was given. It was— *"CHARGE!"*

The battle was on!

Ahead went our three companies of the Seventh Cavalry, direct for the Indians, each man trying to be the first to draw blood.

Never was a more gallant charge made by any troops.

The Second Cavalry had been ordered to round up and look after the ponies of the reds, and this placed the burden of the fight on the three companies of the Seventh Cavalry. The charges on the reds and on their ponies were simultaneous.

Two men reel in their saddles and fall to the ground at the beginning of the charge. There is no faltering, spurs hasten to the utmost the speed of the horses. We soon come to where the ground is so cut up by natural rifle pits that our horses can advance no further. The Indians are firing rapidly; our men are responding.

Halt!—is the shrill bugle command.

Then *Dismount!*—and *Prepare to Fight on Foot!*

And this is what was done, and with as much coolness as though we were on parade, instead of being where bullets are whistling.

As soon as our men dismount the carbines begin to talk to the Indians so fast and with such good results, that the fire of the reds slackens, as they take to cover, but soon they are firing more rapidly than before.

General Miles gave orders for the men to shelter themselves as much as they could and to make their shots count. Men got behind anything that would afford the least shelter, and some dug into the earth with entrenching tools. We lay there and shot at every moving thing seen above the tops of the breastworks of the reds. There are many men in the command who never before were under fire, and they are as aggressive and cool as the veterans.

A man falls on the right of the line—or, rather, rises and then falls! He was lying down when a rifle bullet hit him in the shoulder. He springs to his feet in agony, and instantly falls, and rolls behind a little pile of dirt, and tries to grasp his carbine, but he cannot do so with hands benumbed, and sinks back as though dead!

There he lies until darkness makes it safe for comrades to go to his relief. He was found alive, and taken to the hospital tent on a stretcher, where the Surgeon dressed the wound and he soon became conscious. It is Private Deitline, of Company M. The Surgeon says he is badly wounded, but will pull through all right. Good, for we all like him; he is our Company Farrier.

Other wounded men are taken to the hospital. We soon get over the nausea at first caused by the sight of wounds and blood, and assist in caring for the injured.

The First Sergeant of Company M is found dead, shot through the lungs, while in the front row of little ditches our men had dug in order to press closer to the entrenched Indians; he is the man who declared when bidding his wife and children goodbye, as our force left Fort Rice last Spring, that he had a presentment that they would not see him again.

The body was placed in a grave, over which a volley was fired.

During the battle, Lieutenant Eckerson with a few men distinguished themselves, when horses attached to the mountain howitzer were shot while the piece was being hauled into position. The Lieutenant leaped from his horse, cut the traces, helped the men place the gun in position, and fired shot after shot.

Trumpeter Herwood saved the life of his Captain and thereby came near sacrificing his own. He saw an Indian taking careful aim at the Captain, and deliberately stepped in front of his officer receiving the bullet in his own side. When bringing in the wounded we found Harwood lying on the ridge where he had fallen, and told the Surgeon that the man was so badly wounded that we feared he would bleed to death while being carried to the hospital. Surgeon Harve made examination and said: "He can't live; take in those who have a chance to recover."

The next morning, while being attended to at the hospital tent by Surgeon Havre, Trumpeter Herwood said: "I am the man you left on the ridge to die! If you are going to probe my wound with a finger, as you did last night, please cut the nail off!"

We dug rifle pits, both day and night, and got nearer and nearer the enemy. Chief Joseph's entire camp was surrounded the first day of the fight, but that was not enough to make him yield. He had sufficient food and ammunition for a siege.

On ascertaining this fact, after Chief Joseph had refused to surrender, General Miles had a series of rifle pits dug that cut off the water supply of the reds. Chief Joseph was not slow to discover this fact, and seeing that he could not possibly escape from the trap he was in, or defeat the white force, he held a council at which it was decided to surrender to General Miles! This emphasized their dislike for General Howard, the Department Commander, to whom they attributed the troubles that had started them afield.

6

Sunset of the Horse Soldier

By the 1890s, the glory days of the U.S. Horse Cavalry were over and done. The problem was that nobody seemed to know it. The outrageous and dishonorable behavior of the Seventh Cavalry at the Massacre at Wounded Knee might have been seen as symbolic of this aspect of a proud warrior culture in decline, that what had for a hundred years been a vibrant arm of America's military henceforth would be a matter of inglorious border patrols and shabby police actions. Warfare itself had changed, and the horse soldier's occupation was gone. True, men like Teddy Roosevelt still thirsted for a cavalry charge, but they were living in a dream of the past. The nature of firepower had so developed that the very idea was near to madness. For charging men to have any chance at all they needed to dismount and move forward afoot, as in the Rough Riders' most famous battle.

The Rough Riders at San Juan
Adapted from Edward Marshall's The Story of the Rough Riders, 1st U.S. Volunteer Cavalry

I must start by saying that I did not see any part of the three days' battle of San Juan, and that what is written here is written from what I have been told by men who did, and from what I have read. I have taken considerable trouble to see that every statement is accurate, however, and am convinced that there are few, if any, mistakes in this account.

As everyone knows, the battle started on the first day of July. General Wheeler and General Young were both ill, so General Sumner took command of the cavalry division, in which the Rough Riders were included, in the Second Brigade. This promoted Lieutenant-Colonel Roosevelt to the colonelcy and to command of the regiment, for Colonel Wood became a brigadier-general, and took command of General Young's brigade.

The regiment had moved to El Poso the previous day, and were encamped on that picturesque little farm which the Spaniards had evacuated. Nothing can describe the filthy state in which the retreating soldiers had left the place. "If Cuba is unhealthy, this is what makes it so," said General Sumner to a foreign attache. "New York City would breed yellow fever germs faster than a horse can run, if it were left in such a state as this. When they eliminate unnecessary dirt from Cuba they will eliminate yellow fever."

But the fevers which began to make many a man in the Rough Riders ache and shiver, were not caused by the filth. The days were incredibly hot and the nights were chilly. From the valleys on both sides of the hill where the regiment was encamped, white mists full of the miasma of malaria rose every night to fill the air until the next morning's sun dissipated them, and these mists sent many men to hospital. They added greatly to the beauty of the situation, however, although it is not probable that the Rough Riders were as deeply interested in that as they were in the quinine which was scarce and which this detail of the beauty made necessary.

The order to move forward toward Santiago along the San Juan trail was given the night before to Colonel Roosevelt, who had reveille sounded at three in the morning, for his troops were supposed to be on their way at four. There was a good deal of suppressed excitement among the men. The feeling of security that had preceded the battle of Las Guasimas was replaced by a feeling of wonder and, in some cases, apprehension. The general orders which had been given to their commanders spread among the men with great rapidity, although it is, of course, the military intention that such things shall be known only to the men who must of necessity be confided in. There was no longer any doubt in the minds of the Rough Riders that there were Spaniards in Cuba and that the Spaniards had guns, and that the guns would be loaded and fired, and that they would be fired for the purpose of killing the soldiers in the American army.

I do not wish to give the idea that the Rough Riders were afraid the night before San Juan, for I do not believe that this regiment could have found any set of circumstances which would have made it, as a body, feel afraid. But I do mean that the Rough Riders had learned to take war seriously. They had only to close their eyes to see the battlefield of Las Guasimas where they had so busily passed that morning of the twenty-fourth of June. And in the visions which they thus called to their minds they saw it dotted with prostrate comrades who were not lying down in order to facilitate their own aim at their enemies, but were lying down because they had been hit by Spanish bullets. They could see wounded men all bloody and they could see dead men. They knew that just before the battle those men who were wounded and those men who were dead had felt just as they had felt—had not believed that they would be wounded or dead. And the Rough Riders who brought these pictures to their eyes when they closed them knew that the next day there was going to be another battle and had every reason to believe that after it was over there would be a new list of hurt and killed. And they knew and considered carefully the fact that it was not at all impossible that their own names should be written on it. So they wondered and gossiped among themselves as to who would be hit.

And instead of saying scornfully, "Aw, them Spaniards won't fight," and, "Dagoes can't shoot, anyhow," they polished up their rifles which they had now learned how to use, and they did what they could to prepare to fight ably and manfully against a foe for whom they had achieved a very considerable respect.

It would not be right to say that the men were not sorry to see Colonel Wood taken away from the command of the regiment, but that they were all extremely well pleased over Colonel Roosevelt's promotion is certain. And they could feel that way without hurting anyone's feelings, for they could congratulate Colonel Wood on the fact that he was now a brigadier-general, both by word of mouth and in their minds.

While they had been learning to respect the Spaniards, they had continued to lose their respect for Cubans. The Cuban officers were very largely responsible for this themselves, for they kept up the same policy of boorish indifference to the comfort of the American troops which had distinguished them and surprised us the night we landed at Siboney. And the Cuban soldiers had shown a great tendency to appropriate the property of our soldiers in blue. The sight of American blankets in the possession of Cubans who could not explain where they had got them had ceased to excite surprise, and ugly stories were afloat among the men, of Cuban vandals who had rifled the pockets and bodies of the dead and wounded at Las Guasimas. For some reason or other the Rough Riders, particularly, had conceived doubts about the courage of our Cuban allies, and when it was announced that General Chaffee in his attack upon El Caney would be supported and assisted by a large body of Cuban troops, loud derisive cries were heard in the camp of the Rough Riders. I do not know how Chaffee's men felt about it, nor how General Chaffee himself felt about it, but I am inclined to believe that he had been infected with the same doubts. For he went ahead and prepared for battle exactly as if there were to be no brave and doughty legions of Cuban warriors to help him win, and, later, he went ahead and won just as if there had been none. Exactly as if there had been none, for there were none. That is, the Cuban troops were in the position which had been assigned to them, but they forgot to fire their guns and they forgot to advance on the enemy.

Who planned the position which was given to the Rough Riders on the morning of the 1st of July, I don't know. It indicated a strange disregard of the safety of the regiment which had already shown itself to be one of the best fighting machines that a modern army had ever held. The regiment was halted in the yard of the El Poso farmhouse, and then Grimes's battery was wheeled into position just a little in front of it. Grimes's battery had no smokeless powder. Every shot it fired was followed by a cloud of smoke large enough to furnish a good target even to such inaccurate gunners as the Spaniards.

To the unthinking men in the ranks of the Rough Riders, the presence of the guns was a great comfort. I have heard it said by English officers of eminence, that if it were not for the comfort which the sight and sound of big guns give to the soldier armed with a rifle, and for the terror which the sight and sound of those same big guns inspire in the minds of the enemy, it would not be worthwhile to take artillery on the field except where there were heavy fortifications to be reduced or a siege to be conducted. For statistics show that artillery is by no means proportionately fatal to the enemy with small arms. In other words, the cannon are there for moral effect while the rifles are there for man-killing purposes. The same English officers greatly appreciate the moral effect, however, and have full belief in the necessity of artillery.

The moral effect of Grimes's battery was strong in the Rough Riders, and filled the hearts of them with glee. Grimes's battery fired about nineteen shots before the Spaniards answered. When the answer came, it was directed with excellent aim at the cloud of smoke which hung over and around the American guns, and was, itself, fired with smokeless powder which gave the American guns no target.

Our first shot was fired while the men were eating breakfast. They could plainly see a Spanish blockhouse, and when they observed that either the first or some succeeding shot had struck this blockhouse, they gathered in little groups and they shouted wild western and college yells with the same enthusiasm which afterwards carried them up San Juan Hill. The rejoicing of the Rough Riders over this shot was at the height of its intensity when the first Spanish shell was fired in answer. They heard the shot fired and then they heard for the first time in their lives the awful shriek of a shell's flight. They could not see it, but the growing sound of its advance seemed to come toward them so slowly that they looked against the sky eagerly and anxiously as if they should see the black ball in relief against it. Like the passage of a mammoth sky-rocket, hissing and howling like a fiend of the air, this first Spanish shell came to freeze the grins on the faces of the Rough Riders and to stop midway their screams of excited delight over what our shells had done.

Then the shell exploded with a report which is not like any other report. And when it exploded, it was in the midst of the Rough Riders and, as its smoke cleared away, it exposed to view two dead men, and seven wounded men with the kinds of wounds that were new to the regiment. These were not the clean-cut Mauser holes which had marked the unfortunates at Las Guasimas. They were great jagged rents torn into the quivering flesh by rough-edged fragments of broken steel. And there was no more laughter. And there were no more shouts. War was grim again. More of their comrades were lying dead. The second battle had begun. The Spaniards were really shooting to kill.

It was the first time and the last time, during the campaign, that there was anything like a stampede among the Rough Riders. It was the first time and the last time, during our war with Spain, that they ever yielded an inch to Spanish shots of any kind. But this shell was so unexpected and so dreadful, that the men did not wait for the word of command. They ran scurrying away from the position which they had been ordered to occupy over the edge of the hill to the right, where they showed their newly acquired respect for Spanish gunnery by keeping cover until about half-past eight o'clock. The first shot from the American battery had been fired at six-forty, and the Spanish shell had shrieked its way into their midst at exactly seven o'clock.

While they were at El Poso, a funny episode was the strange maneuver of the First Cavalry. It moved past them with great enthusiasm. It had only a disconcertingly short distance to go before it struck the Spanish outposts, and the Rough Riders knew this. They supposed, of course, that an attack on the foe was intended by the movement. Promptly on time, and exactly at the place where the Spaniards were supposed to be, the First Cavalry ran into them. The Rough Riders were waiting for a battle royal, and more or less expecting that they would soon be involved themselves. But with a promptness which was only equal to the rapidity of their advance, the First Cavalry retired again to some unknown point, and the night grew still and peaceful, and the First Cavalry had marched up the hill, and then marched down again, as did the King of France in the nursery rhyme.

It was nine o'clock before they received their orders to go forward. They had watched many regiments pass along the trail before their turn came, and they shared the experiences of the others when they finally debouched into it. They found it as the others had, muddy, overcrowded, and badly managed. The whole army was moving forward in a line not much wider than the one which the Rough Riders alone had found so inconvenient when they had marched up to Guasimas. I mention this because the army had been inactive for seven days, and had had ample time to prepare for that advance by cutting new trails through the jungle, so that they could have entered the field in half a dozen or a dozen places, instead of in only one place, on which it would have been madness on the part of the enemy if they had not had their guns trained for days. General Chaffee recognized this. But General Chaffee was not in command, so the Rough Riders started down that trail, as other regiments started down that trail, and when ten o'clock came they entered the zone of Spanish fire as other regiments had and did enter the Spanish zone of fire that day. And they could not reply any more than others could reply. And they were 170 wounded and killed helplessly and steadily as the men of other regiments were.

And, with the other troops who were marched needlessly and stupidly into that death trap, they suffered through the madness which sent up a military balloon at a place where the entire American army in Cuba must needs march under it or near it, and catch the terrific fire which the Spanish gunners of course directed at so admirable a target.

They were crossing a creek when they first felt the fire. The water was about two feet deep, and many men were hit while they were wading in it. There was considerable danger that the wounded men who fell in it would be drowned instead of dying pleasantly of their wounds as it is intended that soldiers shall die, and the men who had first-aid packages and who were looking after the wounded as well as they could, had their hands very busily employed.

Colonel Roosevelt rode mounted to the right, and when he saw the terrible slaughter that the balloon was bringing to the men who followed the route marked down for them, he took his men out of it and around to the right so that they avoided the worst of it, perhaps. The regiment finally halted, standing in the creek. The men of D Troop were waist deep and more in the water. The Spanish shells were whistling weirdly overhead and the blundering gasbag was still there, as if it had been a signal shown to let the Spaniards know the position of our men.

For half an hour, the Rough Riders stood waiting there. Many of them had to keep their positions in the creek, and it is not fun to stand for half an hour in water, with the tropical glare of the Cuban sun beating down upon your head, and its no-less-stifling reflection beating up into your face and against your body from the water. If you add to these discomforts the continual arrival of shells fired by hostile men, which ripped and tore the life out of your comrades, while you looked impotently at their suffering and wondered how long it might be before you were hit yourself, you will find that happiness is far distant and agony very near. Yet the irrepressible good spirits of the Rough Riders did not desert them even here. They would have been very much more in evidence if the men had been able to shoot back—if the pleasing consciousness that they were giving Spain as good as she sent had been theirs; but still they laughed and joked and grimly guyed each other.

Their next move was to the woods—the front from which they later charged with their gallant colonel at their head and drove the Spaniards from San Juan Hill.

This march covered a distance which I have heard estimated at half a mile and which I have heard estimated at three miles. Probably the first figure is nearer right than the second. It is particularly surprising and not especially pleasing to the writer to find that no two men see things alike in wartime. My own remembrance of things I saw at Guasimas is as different from the remembrance of other men who saw the same things at the same time as the difference between these two estimates of distance, and the remembrance of a third man sets both myself and the other chap at fault. But all writers of battle history agree that the most frequent errors of those who see battles are on the side of exaggeration. At any rate, whether this march was long or short, everyone agrees that the weather was terrifically hot, and that the Spanish fire was hotter. The country was either clear or covered with low bushes which offered the men no protection whatever, and many of them went down here as they had gone down at Las Guasimas. It seemed harder to be shot here, for not yet were our men able to fire a single answering shot at the Spaniards who were sending those Mausers singing into their ranks. So great was the execution done in this short time, I am told, that the bandages of the first-aid men were wholly exhausted before the men actually reached the front.

The Rough Riders, through Colonel Roosevelt's own good sense, and not through any merit of the orders under which he was acting, avoided the worst place that the American army found that day. They were not among the troops who poured through the opening from that fatal trail down which most of our helpless men went into the plain where the Spaniards had studied out the range and only had to send their unanswered bullets into the mass of soldiers who were huddled there in a confusion which could have only been avoided by not sending them there at all.

Instead he took his regiment well over to the right to about the point in the line which it had been intended that he should occupy, but he did not take them by the route which he had been instructed to follow. When he got them there he placed them in the woods as well as he could. He made his men lie down while he stood up or rode around on his horse. He took every chance there was, while he allowed his men to take as few as possible. He did many things to add to their love of him before they proved it by following him up the hill. But he could not give them the one privilege which they wanted more than they wanted anything else. He could not then give them the order to fire back at the enemy which was killing them as pot-hunters kill wild rabbits. But by and by he gave them all the chance they wanted.

The middle of the day had passed before the men got their chance. And here it is interesting to go over again that little list of Rough Rider records which is now getting so long that it deserves to be spoken of.

The Rough Riders were the first regiment to be organized of all the volunteers.

They raised the first flag raised by the United States army in Cuba.

They fired the first shot fired in anger by the army in Cuba, and they lost the first man shot by the Spaniards.

And now comes the last and best of their record performances. They led the army in the charge up San Juan Hill.

They lay there where Roosevelt had led them, still taking the fire from the Spaniards and still unable to return it, that 1st of July, with as good grace as any troops could have shown under such depressing and disheartening circumstances. Every once in a while, someone among them was shot. It was one of the men who was wounded there who made a remark as his comrades started away, which is likely to go down into the history of the utterances of wounded men.

"Scorch, boys! Scorch!" he said. "My tire's punctured."

The situation was, perhaps, the most exasperating that troops can be called upon to endure. Several regiments were ahead of the Rough Riders, among them the Ninth Regular Cavalry. This regiment is made up of colored men. I counted its Lieutenant-Colonel Hamilton among my dearest friends, and was with his regiment more than I was with any other during the days preceding our departure from Tampa. I know those negro troopers to be brave men, and, indeed, they proved themselves to be among the best soldiers in the United States army, later that same day. Colonel Hamilton was killed in the charge up San Juan Hill, and his men lost very heavily. They were black heroes, every one of them. But they lay ahead of the Rough Riders and did not attempt to go beyond their orders, which were to lie there and wait for someone to tell them from General Shafter to go ahead. That Colonel Hamilton was as brave a man as Colonel Roosevelt, and as brave a man as any man ever was, I do not doubt for a moment, but his regular army training did not stand him in good stead that day. He had been a soldier all his life and he did what a soldier is supposed to do—he did what he was told to do. He had been told to wait. Colonel Roosevelt understood the necessity of obeying orders as well as Hamilton did, but Colonel Roosevelt had not been turned into a fighting machine by years of discipline, and he thought for himself when his superior officers failed to think for him. Colonel Hamilton did not. So Colonel Roosevelt was the hero of San Juan Hill, although the opportunity for heroism had been before Colonel Hamilton just as long as it had been before Colonel Roosevelt. Hamilton, doubtless, saw the necessity for the charge as soon as Roosevelt did, but he waited for some superior to see it too. Roosevelt waited a reasonable time for his superiors to see it, and then he went ahead on his own hook.

I did not see Colonel Roosevelt that day, of course, for I was lying wounded out on the hospital ship *Olivette* off Siboney. But I can call to my mind a picture of him which I know is accurate.

His face was streaming with perspiration and streaked with honest dirt. His famous teeth were prominent and bared constantly by those nervous twitchings of his face which always accompany whatever he says. They were, probably, very often and very grimly closed that day—those teeth—and it is certain that in the excitement of it all he bit his words off with more abruptness and determination than he usually does. And that is saying much. For Roosevelt always talks as if he were trying to give each word a farewell bite before it leaves his mouth, and ends it suddenly with snap. His hair hung in wet wisps down his forehead. Most of the officers in Cuba had their hair cut as short as possible. Roosevelt wore his a little longer than usual. He had on no jacket, and his shirt was soaked with sweat. He did not wear cavalry boots, but had on russet shoes which had wholly taken on the color of Cuban mud, and ordinary cavalry leggings such as are served out to the troops at thirty-one cents a pair. His riding breeches were of khaki, which, when clean, were a pretty soft brown.

But his were not clean. They were wet and they were covered with great spots of Cuban mud and other dirt. It is unlikely that he had taken them off the night before at all. But they were no dirtier than his campaign hat, which was full of holes cut by an obliging trooper for the ventilation of the colonel's head. From the back of it a blue bandana handkerchief with white spots hung down to shield his neck from sun. This the colonel always wore on his hat after the first battle, where he had it tied around his neck. It was the battle flag of San Juan, and I doubt if any man who was at San Juan Hill will ever be able to see one like it without wanting to cheer. Roosevelt had sewed his shoulder straps to his shirt, but one of them had come off and the other hung loosely flopping at one end in imminent danger of being lost as the colonel's wiry shoulder jerked nervously.

I know just how he stood there as he turned to his men and shouted, "We'll have to take that hill," and how they shouted it back along the line, "We'll have to take that hill," and everyone took the colonel's words up and cried, "We'll have to take that hill."

And then they took it.

In front of Colonel Roosevelt's command, as I have said, was the Ninth Cavalry. Hamilton did not move them. Roosevelt, finding them in his way, shouted:

"If you're not going up, get out of my way, for I am."

They made no signs of advancing, so he mounted and rushed into their rear, shouting to them to make way for the Rough Riders. The surprised darkies did not know what to make of this unexpected whirlwind which was pushing and shoving its way through them, but they parted and let it pass. After it had gone by, the colored men fell in with their officers at their head and were the second regiment up the hill. Hamilton was killed in the charge. The officers of the Ninth felt, at first, a little chagrined at what Roosevelt had done, and were inclined to criticize him for it, but this feeling soon gave way to one of honest and outspoken admiration for the man who had had the nerve to set military rules at defiance and whip the enemy in spite of his own superior officers. With the Ninth went two companies of the Seventy-first New York, a regiment of gallant men who have been criticized as the men in the ranks really do not deserve to be criticized, because some of their officers flunked.

Roosevelt went mounted, waving his sword in the air. I fancy he looked a good deal more like the pictures of fighting men charging, than officers very often do. He must have made the kind of a sight that would have delighted the eyes of any of the famous painters of battle scenes.

The ground was uneven and he had to pay some attention to his horse, which slipped and stumbled several times before he reached the barbed-wire fence which, at last, forced the colonel to abandon him. Roosevelt would likely have preferred to go up that hill on foot instead of riding on his horse, for several reasons. Chief of these is the fact that he was the only mounted man on the whole field, and was, therefore, a bright and shining mark for Spanish bullets. Now no man likes to take an unnecessary risk, no matter how willing he may be to expose himself to such danger as legitimately belongs to him in the course of duty. It is not likely that Colonel Roosevelt enjoyed the realization that he was the very biggest target on the whole field of battle for Spanish bullets to be aimed at. Nor was it at all pleasant to have to watch his horse's steps and urge him and encourage him when he wanted to look around, as he could have looked around if he had been walking instead of riding, to see how his men were acting and whether they were following him as rapidly and as closely as he could have wished. But Roosevelt has always been known as a man of lightning thought, and before he mounted at all that day, he realized in a flash that a leader on horseback, brandishing his sword and going like the devil up that hill, would be easier for the men to follow, and more inspiring to them, than a leader walking, who could only go as fast as they could, and who would very likely be so winded by the physical exertion of climbing that he would be unable to shout his orders so that they could be heard.

It has been said that Roosevelt's horse was shot under him that day. This is a mistake. Several officers' horses were shot while their owners were mounted on them before the day was over, but Roosevelt's was not one of these. The animal was hit by a piece of a shell, but the wound was very slight.

The barbed-wire fence was a bad place. It stopped Colonel Roosevelt and it stopped the men who were coming after him. Before that they had straggled along separately and slowly. They could not dash. The hill was too rough, and they were too tired, and the weather was too hot for them to make a wild rush and get there quick. They went up slowly and laboriously. It was mighty hard work. They had no right, according to the ideas of tacticians, to go up that hill as they did, so long as they were not backed up by artillery. But they struggled along without any military formation until they reached this barbed-wire fence. The first men who had wire nippers cut it as quickly as they could, but the pause had been long enough to allow other men to come up, until they were bunched there, and this offered the Spaniards a better chance for shooting than they had had before. They took advantage of it. There were as many men of our regiment hit in that huddle there as were hit in all the places else on the hill put together.

As soon as Roosevelt, now dismounted, had passed the barbed-wire fence he said the only harsh thing which he said to his men during the entire campaign. He turned around and shouted back at the crowd who were toiling along after him:

"If any man runs I'll shoot him myself."

It hurt the men to hear him say such a thing, for there was no one there who had the slightest thought of running. They felt better a moment after when he added, tactfully:

"And I won't have to shoot any of my own men either," but he was sorry he had said anything of the kind, and they were sorry they had heard him, although they all realized that when a man is laboring under such excitement as Roosevelt was at that moment, it is impossible for him to pick and choose his words as he would if he were in a drawing room, or even in a military camp. At any rate, of course no one ran and so Roosevelt did not have to shoot anybody.

Perhaps it is not quite accurate for me to call this part of the battle the "Charge up San Juan Hill," for this hill was not properly a part of San Juan Hill. It was a little preceding hill, and between it and San Juan Hill proper was a slight depression containing a shallow pond of water. At the top of this first hill were some large sugar kettles, so the regiment named it "Kettle Hill," so that in speaking of it they could differentiate between it and San Juan Hill. Here the Rough Riders put in what was, by all odds, the hardest part of their fighting, and lost far more men than they did after they began to ascend the eminence after which the battle is named. The bullets flew like bees around those kettles and like bees they were very busy. But they were not gathering honey. They were spilling blood. Not less than a dozen of the Rough Riders went down here, and several were killed outright. It is said that the fire slackened slightly after our men reached the top of this first hill, and that the Spaniards began to evacuate their main trenches without waiting for us to come further. I could easily devote a chapter to the little incidents which happened at this very part of the charge. But I will limit myself to one.

Captain "Bucky" O'Neill was killed. He had led his troop with great gallantry so far. O'Neill's death was thus described by his first sergeant:

"O'Neill directed us to march at intervals of twelve feet. 'There will be fewer of you hurt.' We went north and then down into the sunken road. It was terrible hot down there, but it was much worse when we got in the open field. Bullets from the blockhouse and from the trenches swept down on us constantly. We came to a barbed-wire fence; it looked as if it were going to stop us, because for some reason none of us who reached it first had wire nippers, but we beat it down with the butts of our carbines, and scrambled over the prostrate wires.

"Then we lay down and fired, but O'Neill stood up straight, and told us not to get rattled, but to fire steady, and kill a Spaniard every time we shot. Then we made a rush. Troop K came up behind us, and we lay down again to fire, but O'Neill walked cheerfully up and down the line talking to us. Lieutenant Kane cried out:

"'Get down, O'Neill. There's no use exposing yourself in that way.'

"O'Neill turned and laughed, and said:

"'Aw-w! The Spanish bullet has not been molded that can hit me!'

"And then one hit him in the mouth and killed him."

Roosevelt led his men down the little descent at the other side of Kettle Hill, still waving his saber and shouting encouragingly at them. Just as they approached the edge of the little pond something—either a bullet or a piece of shell—struck him on the back of the hand and made a slight wound. That moment Roosevelt was the happiest man in Cuba.

He was mighty glad of the wound and, incidentally, probably, mighty glad that it was no worse.

He waved his hand proudly in the air so that the men who were near enough to him could see the blood, and shouted:

"I've got it, boys! I've got it!"

Then he turned to a wounded man who was not far away, and cried, laughingly:

"You needn't be so damned proud."

Through the water of the pond he waded with great strides. Once he stumbled and almost fell, but recovered himself quickly and kept on. By this time the inspiration of the Rough Riders' charge had infected the whole army, and half a dozen regiments were springing forward all along the line. The Spaniards saw this and were frightened. There was never, for a moment, any doubt as to the ultimate outcome of the fight, for the Americans greatly outnumbered their adversaries; but there probably was never a place where in so short a time so many bullets were fired at so few men, as were poured down at the Rough Riders during their charge. But they never flinched. I have been told by a Spanish officer that the Spaniards were so lost in their surprise that they forgot to fire, but if any forgot to fire we did not miss their bullets. Our men were able to get along without them. The whole thing, however, seemed incredible. By this time the men had separated again as they were at first, and each man was picking his own route without making any pretense at keeping alignment or doing anything but get up that hill, firing a shot occasionally when he felt that he could afford the time to stop and shoot, which was not often.

The work was slow—painfully slow. By this time the combination of heat, exertion, and excitement had made the men feel as if they had already done a pretty hard day's work. They struggled and puffed. Once in a while one of them would "get it." The effect of the bullets on that upward slope was curious. Sometimes—when a man was hit in an outstretched arm, for instance, or in the extreme outer shoulder, he would whirl part of the way around before he fell. But fall he would, and since I have seen men fall with Mauser bullets in them, I shall never feel that anyone else I see go down really does the task completely. The shock of such tremendously high-speed projectiles seems to completely paralyze the motor nerves—the nerves which transmit the impulse of contraction and expansion from the brain to the muscles—and thus every muscle becomes instantaneously and completely limp. The men went down, literally, like wet rags. Some of them regained their control over their muscles almost at once, and got up again, either to go on toward those spitting rifle pits at the top of the hill, or else drop back again to the ground from the pain of their wounds. Not one wounded man, so many people who were there have told me, even in his agonies, tried to walk or crawl back towards the rear.

The men took their wounds as cheerfully at San Juan as they had taken them at Guasimas. I have talked with the two first-aid men who probably did more work among the Rough Riders that day than any others, and they tell me the same story of "no complaints" from the wounded. Never in any battle in any land could the men involved have shown a more admirable spirit. Never could they have shown an eye more single to the accomplishment of their duty and more blind to their own pains and hardships.

Up, up, up, they went—slowly, painfully, straining every nerve, cracking every muscle. The sun beat on their heads and made them faint, but valor beat in their hearts and made them strong. It may be because I had been with the Rough Riders when I met my own disaster that I feel so strongly on the subject, but it seems to me this moment as if I would rather have seen that regiment, crawling like warlike ants up that hill from which the little deadly spikes of fire were sending death at them, than to have seen any other sight in all the world.

John Foster, of B Troop, was the only American soldier who came near enough to the Spaniards to make a hand-to-hand fight necessary. He killed one with the butt of his rifle.

The trenches at the top of the hill were literally full of dead enemies. They had had all the advantages of position and entrenchments, but, notwithstanding reports to the contrary, they were greatly outnumbered, and knew from the beginning when they saw our men starting in swarms out of the woods that the battle could have only one result. It does not detract from, but rather adds, to the glory of the fighting done by our men to give the devil his due, and say that the soldiers of Spain showed a dogged courage and grim determination to kill as many Yankees as they could as they hopelessly fired, fired, fired, from their trenches up there—a bravery which was only exceeded in its glory by the dogged persistence of our own men who went up against them.

The objective point of Roosevelt's charge was a blockhouse. Its nasty little loopholes had been spitting fire at him and killing his men during the entire weary, dreadful climb. There were five troopers with him when he reached it. Most of the Spaniards who had occupied it had been killed. All of the others, except one, had run over to the right when they saw our men getting so near that hope was gone. But this one Spaniard stayed where he was, and with a grim, set face, continued to fire. Someone called on him to surrender. He answered with another shot. Roosevelt's revolver was in his hand. He raised it with deliberate aim and killed the Spaniard.

"It was a pity to kill so brave a man as he," he said.

But the work was not over. On the next hill of the little chain, over to the right, the Spaniards who had run away from the one which Roosevelt now held, were with the men who had been there all the time in the trenches. They must be driven back. A little conference was held, and Roosevelt said he would take that hill too. It was agreed that this further advance could only be made at the expense of many lives, and there were those among our officers who did not think the game was worth the candle. Roosevelt was not a halfway soldier any more than he had been a halfway police commissioner, or any more than he is now a halfway governor. He made up his mind to finish the job he had so well begun, and turned to the men who were around him.

"Who'll follow me?" he demanded.

With that he jumped out. For a moment, it looked as if the Rough Riders might have had enough, for only five men sprang in behind him. Three of these fell at once. Roosevelt stood there with but two living followers. He went back.

"I thought you would follow me," he said, terribly grieved.

"We'll follow you to hell!" someone cried out. "We didn't hear you, colonel."

He sprang out once more and there were three hundred men behind him this time.

The spirit of the Spaniards was gone. The terrible Americans were after them again. The task was not a hard one. They fled in terror.

And Roosevelt and his men were on the position which they occupied until the end of the fighting.

Appendix: Daily Life of a U.S. Cavalryman

The Appendix closes our chronicle of exploits with Remington's A Model Squadron. To me, there's something almost heartbreakingly naive in its school-boyish portrayal of the cavalry trooper. It is almost as though the fearsome mounted warrior had become a clubman or amateur athlete.

A Model Squadron

I am not quite sure that I should not say "The Model Colonel," since everyone knows men and horses are much alike when they have first passed under the eye of the recruiting officer and the remount board, and everyone knows that colonels are very unlike, so that a model squadron or a model troop is certain to owe its superiority to its commander; but as we are observing the product in this instance, let the title stand as above stated.

The model squadron aforesaid is quartered across the Potomac from Washington in Fort Meyer, which is the only purely cavalry post in the country. Everywhere else the troops are mixed, and the commandant may be of any arm of the service. Here they are all cavalry, with cavalry officers and cavalry ideas, and are not hindered by dismounted theories, or pick-and-shovel work, or any of the hundreds of things which hamper equally good "yellow legs" in other posts. There are many passable misdemeanors in this post, but only one crime, and that is bad riding. There is little dismounted work, and any soldier can have his horse out on a pass, so long as he does not abuse the privilege; and when he does, it's plenty of walking falls to his lot.

There is a large brick riding-hall of approved pattern, which enables the men to do their work in all weathers. The four troops now quartered there are from the First, Seventh, Eighth, and Ninth regiments, which creates a good-natured rivalry, very conducive to thorough work. It is the opinion of General Henry that one old troop should always be left at this post as a pacesetter for the newly transferred ones, which seems reasonable.

Now to tell what the preparatory discipline is to the magnificent riding which can be seen any morning by spectators who are "game for a journey" to the fort by ten o'clock, I must say that General Guy V. Henry is a flaming fire of cavalry enthusiasm. He has one idea—a great broad expanse of principle—ever so simple in itself, but it is basic, and nothing can become so complicated that he cannot revert to his simple idea and by it regulate the whole. It is the individual training of the horse and rider. One bad rider or one unbroken horse can disarrange the whole troop movement, and "woe to him" who is not up to concert pitch! "Who is the scoundrel, the lummux, humph?" and the colonel, who is a brevet-brigadier-general, strides up and down, and fire comes from his nostrils. "Prefer charges against him, captain!" and the worst befalls. The unfortunate trooper has committed the highest crime which the commandant of Fort Meyer knows— he cannot ride.

A soldier becomes a rider by being bucketed about on a bareback horse, or he dies. The process is simple, the tanbark soft, and none have died up to date, but all have attained the other alternative. This is unimportant; but the horse—it is to his education that the oceans of patience and the mountains of intelligence are brought to bear. It is all in the books if anyone cares to go into it. It is the gathering of the horse; it is the legs carried to the rear of the girths; it is the perfect hand and the instant compliance of the horse with the signs as indicated by the rider; it is the backing, the passaging, the leading with either foot, and the pivoting on the front legs; it is the throwing of horses, the acquisition of gaits, and the nice bitting; it is one hundred little struggles with the brute until he comes to understand and to know that he must do his duty. It all looks beautifully simple, but in practice we know that while it is not difficult to teach a horse, it is quite another matter to unteach him, so in these horses at least no mistakes have been made. After all this, one fine sunny Friday morning the people drove out from Washington in their traps and filed into the galleries and sat down—fair women and brave men; of the former we are sure, and of the latter we trust. The colonel blew a whistle—ye gods, what a sacrilege against all the traditions of this dear old United States army!—and in rode Captain Bomus's troop of the First Plungers, which I cannot but love, since I am an honorary member of their officers' mess, and fondly remember the fellows who are now sniffing alkali dust down in Arizona. They were riding with blankets and surcingles, and did their part of a drill, the sequence of which I have forgotten, since it was divided with the three other troops—Captain Bell's, of the Seventh, Captain Hughes's, of the Ninth, and Captain Fountain's, of the Eighth. I felt a strong personal interest in some of these men, for memory took me back to a night's ride in Dakota with a patrol of the Ninth, when they were all wrapped in buffalo-skin overcoats, with white frost on their lapels; the horses' noses wore icicles, and the dry snow creaked under the tread of the hoofs as we rode over the starlit plain and through the black shadows of the *coulees*. I had pounded along also through the dust in the wake of this troop of the Eighth when it wasn't so cold, but was equally uncomfortable.

The sharp commands of the captain soon put the troop in motion, and they trotted along with a cadenced tread, every man a part of his horse; they broke into fours and wheeled to the right about, then into line and wound themselves up in the "spiral," and unwound again, and soon brought order out of a mess, and the regular canter was ever the same. Then low hurdles were strung across the hall, and by column of fours the troop went over, never breaking the formation; to the rear they turned and back again; finally, they took the obstacle in line, and every horse rose as though impelled by the same mechanism. As if this was not enough, every second man was dismounted and put on double with a comrade, not with his breast to his comrade's back, but back to back, and then in line the odd cavalcade charged the hurdles, and took them every one. It was not an individual bucketing of one horse after another, but all in line and all together. After this what could there be more to test the "glue" in these troopers' seats? There was more, however, and in this wise: the saddles were put on, but without any girths, and all the movements were gone through with again, ending up with a charge down the hall, and bringing up against the wall of the spectators' stand at a sharp "halt," which would have unseated a monkey from a trick-mule.

The horses were all thrown by pulling their heads about, and one cavalryman amused himself by jumping over his prostrate mount. They rode "at will," and stood upon their knees on their horses' backs. One big animal resented carrying double, and did something which in Texas would be called "pitching," but it was scarcely a genuine sample, since the grinning soldiers made little of it.

The troop of the Ninth executed a "left backward turn" with beautiful precision, and this difficult undertaking will serve to give one an idea of the training of the mounts.

Gymnastics of all sorts were indulged in, even to the extent of turning summersaults over four horses from a springboard. A citizen near me, whose mind had probably wandered back to Barnum and Bailey, said:

"But what's this got to do with soldiers; is it not highly flavored with circus?" I could offer no excuse except the tradition that cavalrymen are supposed to ride well. All the men were young and in first-rate physical fix, and seemed to enjoy the thing—all except one old first sergeant, who had been time-expired these half-dozen times, whose skin was so full of bullet holes that it wouldn't hold blood, and who had entered this new régime with many protests:

"O'me nau circus ape; I can't be leppin' around afther the likes av thim!" whereat the powers arranged it so that the old veteran got a job looking after plug tobacco, tomato cans, tinned beef, and other "commissaries," upon which he viewed the situation more cheerfully.

The drill was tremendously entertaining to the ladies and gentlemen in the gallery, and they clapped their hands and went bustling into their traps and off down the road to the general's house, where Madam the General gave a breakfast, and the women no doubt asked the second lieutenants deliciously foolish questions about their art. The gentlemen, some of whom are Congressmen and other exalted governmental functionaries, felt proud of the cavalry, and went home with a determination to combat any one hostile to cavalry legislation, if a bold front and firm purpose could stay the desecrating hand.

But all this work is primary and elementary. The second degree is administered in fieldwork, comprising experimental marches, and those who know General Henry by reputation will not forget his hundred-mile march with the Ninth Cavalry at Pine Ridge, and those who know him personally will become acquainted with his theory that a cavalry command in good condition, with proper feeds, should make fifty miles a day, with a maximum on the road of ten hours a day, moving at the rate of five miles an hour in cavalry halts, the gaits being walk, trot, and leading, with a day's rest each week, to be continued indefinitely. And knowing all this, they will be sure that the model squadron wears out a good many horseshoes in a season.

The "Cossack outposts" are another feature much insisted on, and, strange to say, this arrangement was first invented in America, despite its name (see Wagner's *Outposts*), and is an improvement on picket posts in a ratio of 240 to 324. Another movement is the "form square," which is an adaptation of the "Indian circle," it being a movement from a center to a circle, and useful when escorting wagons or when surprised. The noncommissioned officers are sent on reconnaissance, on patrols, and are required to make maps, which are submitted to an inspector.

Another scheme which I have never seen was the linking of a troop of horses, formed in a circle, to one another, by hooking the regular cavalry links from one horse's bridle to the next one's halter ring, and then leaving them in charge of one man. I also saw the new cavalry bit for the first time. It is commended by all who use it, and I saw no horses boring on it or in the least uppish about going against it, and I never remember a horse who would not do either the one or the other to the old trap which was formerly worn.

Two other curious movements indulged in by this squadron are the firing over horses while they are lying down; and, riding double—the man faced to the rear draws his pistol, and while moving to the rear keeps shooting. It might be useful during a slow retreat, and could be done with the carbine equally well.

This whole enterprise at Fort Meyer is vastly encouraging. As one officer said, "We take no credit for it, since others could do the same if they had riding halls and cavalry officers in command." But there are cavalry officers and there are cavalry officers, and it is not every day one is born. For thirty-five years has the old general sat in a McClellan saddle, and the tremendous enthusiasm of newly joined "sub" still remains. The very thought of a wagon arouses his indignation, and every day the mules are brought into the riding hall, and the men initiated into the intricacies of the "diamond hitch." It takes a past-master to pack a mule in twenty-two seconds, however, and I saw that feat accomplished in General Henry's command.

It is a grand thing for the young men to have this practical training by these old veterans of the civil war and the alkali plains before they go on the retired list. It is well for a young man to know enough not to unsaddle a sweating troop of horses in a broiling sun, and to learn that it makes sore backs; and it is quite important if men can cook rations, and not go up to the skyline of a hill when scouting, and rival the statue of "Liberty Enlightening the World," when it is clearly their business to throw what light they have behind them and not before.

It takes experience to put the sole of a boot back on the upper, when it has fetched loose, with four horseshoe nails, and it is not every man that knows that the place to entrench is on the edge of a cut bank, near water, if one expects ever to get out of a round-up. No one can figure that a recruit will know how many people passed over the road before him, or which way they were going, and it takes a long head and good nerves not to pull a trigger unless the sight is dark on the object when the fight may last all day and probably all night; but all these things are not taught in school. If a horse under him is weakening on a long march in an enemy's country, it is an ignorant fool who uses a spur instead of good sense. That's the time to unload a few dollars' worth of government property. But who can understand the value of a rubber blanket, fifty rounds of ammunition, and a pocket full of grub, with a feed of grain in the bag, but one who has tried it? There are lots of dead soldiers who would have learned these lessons if they had been older. In my opinion, the tremendous box of tricks which Uncle Sam's horses are supposed to carry has put more men afoot than will ever be admitted; but at least the old boot has gone, though there is yet room for an intelligent hand with a jack-plane to shave off that cavalry pack. I am inclined to take what everyone tells me is a "cranky" view on this subject, but let it stand until the next hard campaign, and I hope to be able to be more lucid. Horses are horses, and horses are not made of wood, iron, or by rule of thumb.

To revert to Fort Meyer: it is altogether refreshing; it is worth any one's while to go there and see four troops of cavalry which cannot be beaten, and it is positively exhilarating to meet their creator, a thoroughly typical United States cavalry officer, and I'm bound to say his successor in command has had a hard pace set for him.